James De Mille

The Winged Lion

Stories of Venice

James De Mille

The Winged Lion
 Stories of Venice

ISBN/EAN: 9783337006662

Printed in Europe, USA, Canada, Australia, Japan

Cover: Foto ©Thomas Meinert / pixelio.de

More available books at **www.hansebooks.com**

THE NORWOOD SERIES

Newly arranged Standard Collection of History, Biography, Heroism, and Adventure

Fifty favorites in new series New uniform cover design Attractive dies Fine cloth binding Illustrated Price per volume $1

This series can truly be said to cover the world in its scope, as it chronicles heroic and daring exploits in all climes, told by an exceptionally strong list of authors. In addition we have included the full line of George Makepeace Towle's famous " Heroes of History " and the ever popular Headley biographies. It is just the library to entertain and inform a live boy, and while composed of books that arouse eager interest is wholly free from cheap sensationalism.

1. **Andersen, Hans Christian** — The Sand Hills of Jutland
2. **Armstrong, F. C.** — The Young Middy
3. **Barrows, Rev. William** — Twelve Nights in a Hunter's Camp
4. **Ballantyne, R. M.** — The Life Boat
5. **Brehat, Alfred de** — The French Robinson Crusoe
6. **Cozzens, Samuel W.** — The Young Silver Seekers
7. **Clarke, Mary Cowden** — Yarns of an Old Mariner
8. **De Mill, Prof James** — Among the Brigands
9.   The Lily and the Cross
10.   The Winged Lion or Stories of Venice
11. **Farrar Capt. Charles A. J.** — Down the West Branch or Camps and Tramps around Katahdin
12.   Eastward Ho! or Adventures at Rangeley Lakes
13.   Up the North Branch A Summer's Outing
14.   Wild Woods Life or A Trip to Parmachenee
15. **Frost, John, LL.D.** — Wild Scenes of a Hunter's Life
16. **Hall, Capt. Charles W.** — Twice Taken A Tale of Louisburg
17. **Harley, Dr.** — The Young Crusoe or Adventures of a Shipwrecked Boy
18. **Headley, P. C.** — Facing the Enemy The Life of Gen. Wm. Tecumseh Sherman

LEE and SHEPARD Publishers Boston

THE NORWOOD SERIES -- Continued

LEE and SHEPARD Publishers Boston

LOST IN VENICE. — Page 182.

THE WINGED LION;

OR,

STORIES OF VENICE.

BY

PROF. JAMES DE MILLE,

AUTHOR OF "THE B. O. W. C.," "THE BOYS OF GRAND PRE SCHOOL,"
"LOST IN THE FOG," "FIRE IN THE WOODS," "PICKED
UP ADRIFT," "THE TREASURE OF THE SEAS,"
"AMONG THE BRIGANDS," ETC.

ILLUSTRATED.

BOSTON
LEE AND SHEPARD PUBLISHERS
1899

CONTENTS.

CHAPTER I.

CHAPTER II.

CHAPTER III.

CHAPTER IV.

CHAPTER XIX.

CHAPTER XX.

CHAPTER XXI.

CHAPTER XXII.

CHAPTER XXIII.

CHAPTER XXIV.

III.

THE WINGED LION;

OR,

STORIES OF VENICE.

CHAPTER I.

*A rash Plan. — A mournful Separation. — Truant Boys.
— Breaking Faith. — A Surprise. — The beautiful Stranger. — Clive and David find themselves the chosen Pro-
tectors of Beauty in Distress.*

AFTER spending a few weeks in Florence,
Uncle Moses and his young friends began
to discuss the important question of their
next movements; and here a difficulty arose which
led to many odd adventures. As for Uncle Moses,
that worthy man would gladly have left Italy altogether, and gone on as fast as possible to his destination; but the very hint of such a thing roused
so great a storm of opposition and reproach that
he did not press it further. Leave Italy, indeed!
That was not to be thought of. They had many
places still to visit, and many adventures still to
encounter. Bologna, Ferrara, Padua, Milan, Turin,

Genoa,—all these cities lay before them; and greater than all, one which drew them onward with a stronger fascination. For of all the cities of the old world none had ever seemed so attractive and so wonderful as Venice. Its unique situation; its romantic history; its splendid monuments; its canals, gondolas, towers, and palaces; its dark secrets; its alluring mystery,—all served to throw a spell over their minds.

There was but one opinion, therefore, among the boys as to Venice; but their views were widely different as to the time of starting. Frank and Bob preferred waiting in Florence for another week, and then going straight to Venice without stopping at the intervening cities; Clive and David, on the other hand, much as they loved Florence, were anxious to visit Bologna, Ferrara, and Padua. Prolonged argument only made each side more eager in the assertion of its own preferences. The question was argued long and hotly, and only ended in each side maintaining its own view, and blaming the other for obstinacy.

David and Clive talked the matter over, and at length came to an important decision. This was, to go on ahead, leaving the others behind. They could then visit the intervening cities, and afterwards they could all join one another at Padua or Venice. But to this plan it was first necessary to obtain Uncle Moses' consent.

No sooner was it mentioned than Uncle Moses

burst forth with exclamations of amazement and
horror. "To separate!" he cried. "Never!"
He declared that it would be ruin to all of them,
and that his anxiety would be the death of him.
Clive and David were prepared for this refusal;
so they waited patiently till the first storm had
passed, and then returned to the charge. They
teased and coaxed, and tried to show their timid
relative that his fears were groundless. Frank
and Bob thought it a good idea, and magnani-
mously joined the others in their efforts to persuade. Before this combined attack Uncle Moses
grew more yielding, and at length, in a moment of
weakness, was rash enough to give something like
an assent.

But in assenting to their proposal he made some
stipulations. One was, that they should not go
farther than Bologna. Another was, that they
should all join one another in two or three days.
These terms were agreed to, and Clive and David
in great glee began to prepare for their departure.

But in the mind of Uncle Moses there was something very different from glee. No sooner had his
reluctant assent been wrung from him than heavy
clouds of anxiety began to roll over that good
man's gentle heart. He repented greatly, and
tried to dissuade them. He told them that they
were too young, and that they could not be
trusted alone on such a journey. To this Clive
and David replied with a laugh, and informed

Uncle Moses that he was the only one of the party who was in any danger when alone.

And so there was, on the side of Uncle Moses, a very mournful parting.

"You'll be sure and take care of yourselves, dear boys," he wailed forth, as he bade them good by at the station.

"O, yes," was the cheery reply; "and mind, Uncle Moses, don't you go and get into trouble."

These were their last words: the train rolled off, and Uncle Moses went back to his lodgings with his heart full of sadness, and his mind full of dismal forebodings.

The two boys felt full of delight at thus starting off alone. Their minds were full of a glorious sense of freedom; and the only check upon their joy was the thought that this freedom was to be of such short duration. Still they determined to make the most of it while it lasted; and with this laudable design they began, even in the railway carriage, to give vent to their exuberant spirits, to the slight surprise of other passengers. They sang songs; they screamed; they made gestures; they told stories; they quoted poetry; and every minute made some plan which, on the following minute, was superseded by another new one. In this frame of mind they reached Bologna.

On stepping forth from the cars they found, to their disappointment, that the weather had changed. The brilliant sunshine and deep blue skies of Florence were no longer to be seen. Instead of this, they saw overhead nothing but dull, leaden-colored clouds, while a thick drizzle filled the air. As they went to the hotel, they saw that Bologna was a gloomy city, with dull-gray houses and narrow streets, and with nothing whatever to alleviate this depressing exterior. However, they struggled against their feelings of despondency, and after dinner they went out to see the town.

Two or three hours' walk in a drizzling rain, and visits to dreary churches, did not reconcile them to Bologna. On their return to the hotel, they both came to the opinion that Bologna might be a very good place for sausages, but that it was a very mean place for tourists. The prospect of waiting here for three long days was most miserable; so miserable, indeed, that they thought of going back to Florence.

It was David who first proposed another plan. That plan was to go on to Ferrara.

"It's a magnificent city," said David; "full of palaces and historical associations. There Tasso lived, and Ariosto. Let's go there."

"But we promised Uncle Moses to wait at Bologna," objected Clive.

"Certainly," said David. "We'll come back here again, and meet them. But just now, instead of staying in this gloomy hole, it will be a great deal better to spend the time in some decent place."

"That's a fact," said Clive. "It'll be all the same, of course, to Uncle Moses."

"Of course," said David; "he merely wants to meet us here."

So they agreed upon this, and the next morning went on to Ferrara full of high hopes.

On reaching Ferrara they found themselves in a dreary city, with wide grass-grown streets, on which but few people were visible. There was a depressing dullness about the place, against which it was impossible to struggle. Added to this was the hateful drizzle which had followed them as if on purpose to disappoint and humiliate them. They tried to keep up their spirits, but in vain. They visited the churches, they looked with lack-lustre eyes at the cell of Tasso, and strolled languidly through the Museum. After this they went to the railway station, as though the most attractive place in Ferrara was the way that led out of it. Here they studied the time-tables, and neither said a word.

"At two o'clock." said David, suddenly, "the train goes through for Padua."

"Well," said Clive.

"I wonder why we mayn't go to Padua," said David, innocently. "We can stay the night, and come back to Bologna to-morrow, and meet Uncle Moses.'

"Will Uncle Moses leave Florence to-morrow?"

"No, not till the day after. We were to have three days, and he would leave on the fourth."

"Well," said Clive, "we may as well be in Padua as in Ferrara."

"A great deal better," said David. "For my part, I can't stand this place any longer. It's worse than Bologna."

"Ten times worse," said Clive.

The boys now went back to the hotel, got their little valise, which contained all their luggage, and then, returning to the station, waited for the train. It came in due time, and so they soon found themselves in Padua. But although they had hoped for some better fortune in this city, they were doomed to disappointment. The drizzling rain still continued, and they had grown so weary of churches and museums that they did not care to visit any more. They strolled through the streets till they were tired, and finally took refuge in the magnificent Café Pedrocchi, where they ordered a sumptuous dinner, and whiled away the time till dark.

Over this repast they began to grow refreshed, and amused themselves with discussing the situation.

"And so," said David, "we have to go back tomorrow. Well, all that I can say is, we've had a mean sort of excursion."

"It'll never do to own up to Frank and Bob," said Clive. "We must hold our tongues."

"I dare say they've had no end of fun," said David, gloomily. "Florence is such a perfect paradise. What fools we were!"

2

There was a silence for a time, in which each one meditated over his late folly.

"I say, Dave," said Clive, at length.

"What?"

"Suppose we go on to Venice."

"What!" cried David, in amazement.

"The fact is," said Clive, "I've been thinking about it all day."

"Well, for that matter," said David, "so have I."

"You see," said Clive, "Bologna is such a horrible place that I never want to see it again."

"No more do I."

"I'd rather wait here than go back. But since we are here, why, we might as well go on at once to Venice."

"But what'll Uncle Moses do?"

"O, we can write him."

"Where? At Bologna?"

"No; Florence. He won't leave till the day after to-morrow. We can write to-night. He'll get our letter to-morrow. We'll tell him all about it, and where we are going."

"Capital!" cried David. "I thought of Venice, too; but somehow it didn't seem fair to Uncle Moses. Of course his anxiety is only his timidity. We can go round the world safe enough. If we write him, it will be all that is wanted. He may just as well meet us at Venice as at Bologna."

"Of course," said Clive; "and then, you know, neither Frank nor Bob wants to go bothering about these stupid towns. They'll be glad to have it all settled in this way. And Uncle Moses'll be just as glad as the others, for he thinks every town that he misses so much gain for himself. We're almost as near at Venice as at Bologna; and we'll save them from a fit of the blues."

That night the boys concocted a letter. Clive wrote it. The letter was not very long. It gave a brief account of their proceedings, and of their intention to go to Venice. They mentioned a hotel, the name of which they learned from their landlord; and in this way they arranged everything for Uncle Moses, so that he could find them without any difficulty. They knew that they were violating the strict letter of their promise to Uncle Moses, but they thought that they were keeping it in a general way, and that it would be all right so long as they had arranged to meet at the specified time. After all, Venice would be a better place for their reunion than Bologna.

That night they mailed the letter, and the next day they were rolling away in the train for Venice, which was only forty miles away.

On entering the train they found themselves in a compartment with two others — a gentleman and a lady. The lady was very young and exceedingly pretty, with a very sweet face and a profusion of blonde hair. She looked rather sad, and both the boys felt themselves drawn towards the beautiful stranger with feelings of deep sympathy. She did not look like an Italian, but rather like an English lady; or still more, like an American. What made them take a deeper interest in her was the fact that she looked at them very earnestly, and seemed as though she would like to speak to them.

The other passenger was a young man with a fine frank face, dark hair rather long, and dark eyes, which rested occasionally on the boys with a glance of kindly sympathy, mingled with mirthfulness. The lady and the gentleman were evidently not acquainted, for they were seated at a distance from one another, and on opposite sides of the compartment. David and Clive took the middle seats, sitting opposite to each other, and Clive was thus brought within sight of the lady.

This lady looked at him very often, and very fixedly, occasionally stealing a glance at David. Clive admired her face very much. She was evidently very young, for her face was girlish, and she had a timid way about her which made him wonder.

At last the lady leaned forward and spoke to him.

"Do you know anything about Venice?" she asked, in a sweet, low voice.

"O, well, not *very* much," said Clive, wishing to be of assistance to her, and not caring to confess his ignorance. From the tone of her voice Clive knew at once that she was an American lady, and so his interest in her grew stronger than ever.

" If there is anything that I can do," he added, " I shall be very happy indeed."

" You are from America ? " said the lady.

" Yes," said Clive, " from Boston."

" O, 1 am so glad ! " said she. " I've been so awfully frightened ! and I am yet. I was going to Venice with my aunt. We left Milan early this morning. She got out at Verona for something, and told me not to leave the train till she should come back. I waited — when suddenly the train left. My poor aunt did not come. She must have been left behind. At first I thought of getting out at the next station, and going back ; but, then, I don't know Italian, and I thought that dear auntie would come after me. I was dreadfully terrified and confused, and so I've been coming on, with a vague idea of waiting for her at Venice. It seems to me that it will be the wiser course."

" O, yes," said Clive, who was fuller of sympathy than ever, " I should think that it was your best plan."

" We know of a very nice hotel at Venice," chimed in David. " We are going there to wait for our friends, who are coming to join us to-morrow."

" And you can stay at the same place," said Clive, " and wait for your aunt."

" It's the Hotel Zeno," said David. " It's a very comfortable hotel. Our landlord at Padua recommended it highly."

"O, thank you very much," said the lady: "I'll go with you. I'm very glad that I've met with you. You remind me of my two dear little brothers at home. I'm not a bit troubled about myself, but I'm so dreadfully worried about poor dear auntie: for, you know, she doesn't know anything about travelling, and I'm afraid she'll go out of her senses when she finds herself left behind, and separated from me."

"O, well," said Clive, "I'll tell you what we'll do: we'll send back telegrams immediately."

The mention of telegrams seemed to give great relief to the little lady. She thanked them, and told them that they had taken a great load off her mind. And now they all chatted together like children. For the young lady was herself but just out of girlhood, and had all the simplicity and innocence of that sweet season. Clive and David were charmed beyond all expression by her lovely face and her winning ways. They grew rapidly intimate, as boys and girls generally do, and Clive and David told all about themselves, and their new friend told all about herself.

Her name was Gracie Lee. She insisted that they should call her by her Christian name.

"If you were grown-up young men," said she, "I should not have dared to speak to you; but you are boys, and you are so like my little brothers that when you came in I could have cried for joy. And I'm not so very much older than you, either; so I'll pretend that you are my brothers, Fred and Harry, only I'll call you by your own names."

All this was delightful to such romantic boys as Clive and David. Here was an adventure far different from their old ones: this lovely little stranger, who looked out at them so sweetly with her blue eyes, and dimpled cheeks, and golden hair. They were all young and fresh, and unspoiled by the world; and being thrown upon one another in this way, it made them feel like old friends. Gracie felt all her anxiety removed; and Clive and David had a fine sense of responsibility, for Gracie had thrown herself upon their protection, and looked to them to find her lost relative. This, of course, they both felt sure of doing.

CHAPTER II.

*A new Friend. — The young Artist. — A strange Railway
Station. — A wonderful City. — The Grand Canal. —
The Winged Lion. — A Story of St. Mark the Evangelist.
— Pleasant Lodgings.*

THE young man who was sitting opposite to
David had heard every word of the conversation, and had at times stolen glances at
the sweet face of Gracie Lee, without venturing,
however, to intrude himself upon her. At length,
as David's eyes wandered about, he caught sight
of the stranger, who was looking at him with a
careless smile.

"You have never been in Venice before — have
you?" said the stranger.

"No," said David, who could not help taking a
liking to the young man, both on account of his
face and the tone of his voice.

"It's rather an awkward place to land in," said
the other. "I'm an old inhabitant, and if there's
anything I can do, why, I can only say I shall be
very glad to do it."

"Why, you must be an American," said David,
in surprise, as his ear detected the beloved intona-
tions and accent of his native land.

" O, yes," said the young man, with a laugh, " I was born under the shadow of the State House, and was raised in the Boston Latin School. I'm an artist — living here with my mother. I've been living in Venice two or three years — studying Titian, you know."

" How splendid ! " said David, to whom an artist studying Titian seemed almost like an angelic being.

Gracie stole a shy look at the stranger, and then whispered to Clive, —

" How funny ! He's from Boston, too ! "

" My name," said the stranger, " is Vernon — Paul Vernon. I know yours already, you know, as you've been mentioning it ; and if you're going to stay at Venice for any length of time, why, perhaps you would like to see the city. I'll give you my address, and show you the sights."

David was delighted at this. What guide could be equal to an artist — and an American? He thanked Vernon very emphatically. Vernon went on talking in a very pleasant way about Venice, and David liked him better and better every moment. So David and Vernon talked, while Gracie and Clive carried on another conversation by themselves; yet both heard every word that Vernon said.

At length they reached Venice. Vernon informed David that he would get a boat, and that he would go with them as far as the Hotel Zeno. This was not altogether intelligible to David, who thought rather of taking a cab: but soon his meaning was apparent. For on emerging from the station, the party found themselves not on a street, but a canal: while before them there was a large number of gondolas, with that peculiar shape which had become familiar to their eyes from pictures. Some of these were of large size, and had the word *Omnibus* painted on the outside. All the rest were painted black, and had a little cabin at the stern, with a canopy over it formed of black cloth. One of these Vernon had engaged.

"I hope you will pardon me, Miss Lee," said Vernon, approaching Gracie with a pleasant smile, "if I do not stand upon ceremony. But in the cars I couldn't help hearing what you said; and as I know all about this country, it occurred to me that I could be of service to you towards finding your aunt. I know the chief of police here, and I can get them to send off messengers to Verona — that is, if your aunt does not turn up. Meanwhile I can make myself useful by showing you where the hotel is. My mother is living here, and I think she knows some of your people in Boston, and I'm sure you would like to see her. You know Venice is like a ship at sea, and we Americans who live here always feel our hearts grow warm towards any of our fellow-countrymen."

It was quite evident that Vernon's last words were true as far as regarded one at least of the people of his native land; for his heart did certainly feel an unusual warmth as he spoke to his fair young fellow-citizen. As for Gracie, she seemed much pleased.

"O, thank you," said she; "that will be very nice indeed, if you really could manage to send some one."

"O, I'll manage it," said Vernon, eagerly; "for that matter, I'll go myself. So you need not give yourself any further anxiety. Think of Italy as though it were Massachusetts. Travelling here is just as safe, and easy, and simple, as there. Your aunt will be well cared for wherever she is, and I hope that you will find yourself well cared for, too."

Gracie felt very grateful, and could not help thinking that it was very fortunate for her to have found some one who was so well able to hunt up her lost aunt. Vernon's manner, too, was so cordial, so devoted, and withal so respectful, that her natural timidity was quickly dispelled, and she found herself talking with this new acquaintance with the utmost ease and confidence.

Soon they were all in the boat, and moving along through this wonderful city. The first thing that they noticed was the marvellous stillness around them. In other cities there are always the noise of wagons passing over stone pavements, the cries of people, and the confused murmur formed out of all the aggregated sounds of a busy multitude. But here there was nothing of the kind. All was still. The streets were streets of water. Water was the pavement. Over this glided all the people in boats, noiselessly. Foot-passengers, carriages, wagons, carts, horses, all the varied modes of transportation common to other cities, were here reduced to one uniform fashion — the fashion of rowing in boats. The gondoliers stood and propelled the boats by pushing with their oars. The streets were real streets, after all; for on each side rose lofty houses, whose windows looked out upon these streets, as in other cities. Their doors opened out on the street also; but here, if one wished to leave his house, he had to step from the front door into a gondola.

In this way they passed along. Other boats were going in the same direction. All was silent, and the silence was never broken by any sound, except at times, when, on turning a corner, the gondolier would utter a peculiar cry, to give notice to any boat that might be coming from an opposite direction.

"I say, Dave," said Clive, "this sort of thing is a little ahead of Bologna, and Ferrara, and Padua."

"I bet it is," said David, who enjoyed the situation as much as Clive.

At length the gondola shot out from a narrow canal into one which was four times as broad as any which they had thus far seen. The view here was magnificent. On either side rose stately mansions, whose marble fronts were displayed with lavish adornments, and in richly decorated styles of architecture. Boats passed up and down, enlivening the scene. In the distance, above the tallest houses, rose a lofty tower.

"I know this place," said Clive. "It must be the Grand Canal."

"Yes," said Vernon, "you are right. There's nothing like this in any other city."

At length the boat stopped before a mansion, whose marble front, adorned with splendid decorations, rose for many stories above them. Marble steps afforded an entrance from the gondola, through a lordly portico, into the mansion.

"Is this the Hotel Zeno?" asked Clive.

"Yes," said Vernon. "It was once the Zeno Palace; but most of the Venetian palaces are now hotels and boarding-houses; and the name of the greatest of all the Venetian heroes is now fallen to this. But such is life.

> 'Imperial Cæsar, dead and turned to clay,
> May stop a hole to keep the wind away.'

And so most people now only think of Carlo Zeno in connection with this hotel."

They now entered, and all were shown to very handsome apartments. Vernon went away, promising to see them again before long.

He kept his promise. Before an hour had passed he was back again. This time he brought with him an elderly lady, whom he introduced as his mother. She had a soft, low voice, and a sweet and gracious face, which at once gained their hearts. Gracie especially felt the quiet charm of this dear old lady, and before long they were wandering in thought far away, and Mrs. Vernon was telling Gracie of her past life in Boston, and asking after Boston news. Vernon talked with the boys, but kept his ears and eyes open, and noticed everything that Gracie said or did.

And now a new arrangement was made. Mrs. Vernon insisted that Gracie should go home with her, and stay with her until her aunt should come to Venice. A young girl like Gracie, she said, should not be left alone without friends in a great hotel. Her persuasions were not without effect. Gracie herself felt a little timid at the idea of being all alone, with no friends except Clive and David, and Mrs. Vernon seemed to her like a mother. And so, with many apologies and excuses, she at last accepted the kind invitation. Meanwhile Vernon had been giving the same invitation to the boys. At first they declined with many thanks; but Vernon was so urgent that at last they accepted it, and at length the whole party retired from the Hotel Zeno.

And now, once more in a boat, they passed down the Grand Canal, which presented a more striking appearance as they went on. At length the canal broadened into a wide expanse of water; and close by, on their left, they saw a landing-place, which seemed to lead to a great square. Here very many gondolas were drawn up, and just beyond, two lofty pillars arose: one of which was surmounted by a statue of a man, and the other by a statue representing a Winged Lion. Beyond this they saw that same lofty tower which had met their gaze far up the Grand Canal, and in the distance a row of magnificent edifices. Bordering on the canal, a little farther on, there was a stately palace, and behind this, fronting on the inner square, was a cathedral with many domes.

"This," said Vernon, "is the Piazza of St. Mark; and just here, near the pillars, is the Piazzetta, or little square. That is the Ducal Palace: that church with the domes is the Cathedral of St. Mark, and the tower belongs to it, although it stands apart from it, as is often the case in Italy."

"What is that Winged Lion?" asked Clive.

"That," said Vernon, "is the Lion of St. Mark. It is the symbol of Venice — like the British Lion, the symbol of British power — or like the American Eagle, our own majestic fowl. The Winged Lion was once a powerful beast, and was respected all over the Mediterranean, when the British Lion was but a small animal, and long before the American Eagle was hatched."

"I'm afraid," said Gracie, shyly, "that you are just a little bit flippant. It seems like irreverence to call these glorious symbols fowls and beasts."

"Then I'll never call them so again as long as I

live," said Vernon, with an absurd air of contrition,
which made them all laugh; "and I'm sure I didn't
mean any harm."

"But what is the meaning of a Winged Lion?"
asked Gracie. "No lion has wings."

"That's the very question," said Vernon, "that
an Austrian ambassador once asked of a Venetian.
Now, you know the Austrian symbol is a double-
headed eagle; and do you know what the Venetian
replied?"

"No," said Gracie; "I'm sorry to say I'm awfully
ignorant. My education has been frightfully neglected."

"Well," said Vernon, "the Austrian asked the
Venetian in what part of the world winged lions
are found; and the Venetian replied, in the same
country where they have double-headed eagles."

"Well done for the Venetian," said Clive.

"O, it wasn't a very clever thing to say," said
Vernon. "I only tell the story because it's one of
the regular things that one has to say to every new
visitor."

"But why did they take a Winged Lion for their
symbol in the first place?" asked Gracie.

"Ah, well," said Vernon. "'Thereby hangs a
tale.'"

"O, tell it, tell it by all means," said Gracie.
"I'm awfully fond of stories."

Vernon laughed in his usual pleasant fashion,
and began: —

" Well, you know, in the first place, the lion belongs to St. Mark. It has been taken for his symbol ever since the time of the apostles. The reason of this is, that the vision of Ezekiel, where he sees the cherubim, you know, describes them as having four faces, or, as some say, four distinct forms; that is, a man, a lion, an ox, and an eagle. Now, these have always been taken by the church to represent the four evangelists — the man representing St. Matthew; the lion, St. Mark; the ox, St. Luke; and the eagle, St. John."

" O, I'm very glad to know all that," said Gracie. " I'm sure I never heard it before. And that is why St. Mark has the lion. Well, as an American, I feel inclined to take St. John as the patron saint of our country, for his emblem is the eagle. But how did St. Mark's lion happen to have wings?"

" Well, that arose," said Vernon, " from the vision of the prophet Daniel. In his vision he sees four living things — the same as Ezekiel — a man, a lion with eagle's wings, an ox, and an eagle. These also were taken to represent the evangelists; and so, you see, the Lion of St. Mark gained a pair of wings, which wings you may see on that statue."

" How did Venice happen to choose St. Mark for its patron saint?" asked Gracie. " Why not St. Peter? or St. Paul? or St. Bartholomew? For my part, I've always had a weakness for St. Bartholomew. It's such a nice name, you know."

3

Vernon laughed again. "Bartholomew!" said he. "Why Bartholomew more than Nathaniel? The names belonged to the same man. Bartholomew means the son of Tolmaeus, or Tholemew, and that party was Nathaniel's father."

"Well," said Gracie, "I think it's a shame. I've been going to Sunday school all my life, and nobody ever told me all that. But how do you happen to know so much about church history? Why, you ought to write one for the use of Sunday schools. But never mind. Go on and tell how the Venetians happened to choose St. Mark."

"St. Mark, you know," began Vernon, "according to legend, which is very likely to be true, died at Alexandria, and was buried there. His tomb was much revered by the Christians, who believed that miracles were wrought there. After the Mohammedans captured the place, the Christians still kept up their reverence, and at length the Mohammedans also caught the superstition, and used to bring their sick friends there to be healed. At last, one of the Mohammedan rulers, who did not believe in St. Mark, being in want of marble for a new palace, determined to destroy his church, and appropriate the stones for his own purposes. The priests were in a great way. They were afraid that the remains of the apostle would be desecrated, and the lower orders generally were equally afraid of losing the relics which wrought such miracles. So the governor promised to transfer the remains to some other place.

" At that very time there happened to be a number of Venetian ships in port, and the captain of one of them, hearing of what was going on, determined to try to secure the sacred relics of the apostle for his own city. So he had an interview with the priests who had charge of the tomb; pointed out the dangers that would always threaten the grave of a Christian saint among a Mohammedan population; and how desirable it would be to have the body transferred to a safer place: a large bribe was added to the arguments, and all together were so persuasive that the priests consented.

" The work, however, was not easy. The worshippers were numerous, and might detect the act. At length they made an opening in the lower part of the coffin, through which they removed the body of St. Mark, and immediately afterwards put in its place the body of another saint, who, however, was of inferior grade. This removal was attended by a very wonderful circumstance. For no sooner had the body of St. Mark been brought forth into the open air than an odor was wafted forth from it, through all the surrounding space, of such exquisite sweetness that all who came near the church were amazed and delighted at the heavenly fragrance. Inquiries were made, and the tomb was narrowly inspected; but none of the examiners were able to detect any difference. Thus they succeeded in removing the body from the tomb.

" The next trouble was about getting it on shipboard. This was effected by an ingenious device. The body was wrapped up so as to look as little like a human form as possible, and then, as it was carried through the streets, men went before it crying out, 'Pork! Pork!' Now, as pork is an unclean thing among Mohammedans, and an object of horror, those whom they encountered were far more eager to get out of the way than to examine the precious bundle.

"A further trial yet remained. A search was always made by the city police before any ship was allowed to leave port, so as to see that no runaway slaves should escape, and no prohibited articles of commerce be taken away. There was great danger that all their troubles might prove fruitless, since such a thing as the body of an evangelist would be discovered only too easily. But the wits of the Venetian captain were again able to devise a means of escape. He caused the body to be rolled up inside the sail, which was then furled close to the yard-arm. In this way it eluded all examination, and even suspicion. This was the last of the great trials, and nothing further happened until St. Mark arrived in safety at that city which was thenceforth to be forever associated with his name.

"The joy of the Venetians at this great acquisition was unbounded. All the city turned out to receive the precious remains. The doge, and all the chief nobles, the clergy, the entire population, came to do him honor. Solemn services were held, accompanied with the pomp of magnificent ceremonies, and splendid processions, and feasting, and music, and universal joy. St. Mark was taken as the patron saint of Venice. His lion — with eagle's wings — became her symbol, and the battle-cry of her warriors was to be the name of the saint.

" So there is the lion ; and they used to have a very interesting fashion : in peace an open book was placed under his paws ; but in time of war the book was removed, and a drawn sword placed there in its stead."

While they had been looking at the Piazza, with its edifices and towers, and Vernon had been talking, the boat had stopped ; but now it resumed its progress, and before long they came to their destination. It was a lofty house, at a corner where one of the canal streets ran up from the Grand Canal. Here they landed, and went up to a handsome suite of apartments in the second story, from the windows of which there was a magnificent view of the harbor and the suburbs of the city.

" If you will give me your aunt's address," said Vernon to Gracie, " I will go off at once and get the police to see about her."

" O, thank you," said Gracie, earnestly. " I shall feel so much relieved ! "

She then wrote down in Vernon's pocket-book the name of her aunt : —

Miss Lee,

Boston, Mass.

Vernon now hurried off, and was gone about an hour.

"You need give yourself no further anxiety," said he on his return. "The police will send a messenger by the first train to-morrow, and at the same time they will keep a record of all who arrive in the city, and let me know."

This information filled Gracie with delight. She felt confident now that she would soon see her aunt.

CHAPTER III.

*St. Mark's and its Wonders. — The Story of the Demon
Ship. — The Great Barbarossa. — The Artist's Home. —
The two mysterious Pictures.*

FTER taking lunch they all set forth to see
the city, and first of all they went to the
Piazza of St. Mark.

Here they saw a spacious square surrounded by
magnificent edifices. The lofty tower of St. Mark
arose three hundred and fifty feet in the air. The
Ducal Palace, with its long front adorned with pillars and arches, displayed its noble dimensions,
and opened before them those dread portals which
in former ages were the avenue to so much mystery and iniquity. The three tall flag-staffs lifted
to heaven, not the Lion of Venice, nor the Double
Eagle of Austria, but the banner of regenerated
Italy. But the pride and glory of the Piazza, and of
all Venice, was the magnificent Cathedral of St.
Mark, and it was to this that Vernon first conducted
them.

They saw a splendid edifice built of white marble, and crowned with a cluster of swelling domes,
which gave it an appearance rather of Aladdin's

Palace than of a Christian church. The whole front was ornamented with an immense number of columns, formed of every kind of precious marble, polished so as to show the richest and most gorgeous colors. They saw five noble portals opening into the Cathedral, and over each a vaulted recess that blazed with gold, whereon were mosaic pictures wrought in the most brilliant tints. Immediately over the chief portal they saw a deep recess, in which stood four bronze horses, — emblems not of the peaceful services of religion, but rather of the proud achievements of war, and carrying the mind back from the modern republic of Venice to the ancient republic of Rome.

Entering, they found the interior fully corresponding with the promise of the exterior. Everything seemed to blaze with gold and brilliant coloring. The floor, the walls, the vaulted roof, the lofty domes, were all covered with mosaic pictures wrought on gilded background. David and Clive had seen St. Peter's, and therefore were not so deeply impressed by all this splendor as Gracie. She had never yet seen anything half so gorgeous, and was loud in her expressions of admiration.

"How did the Venetians happen," she asked, at length, "to lavish such an enormous amount of treasure on St. Mark?"

"O, why, I'm sure they had every reason to do so," said Vernon. "He was their patron saint. He gave them victory by land and sea. They gained all this by these victories, and the least they could do was to give some of it to him."

"It seems to me rather a funny thing for a saint and an evangelist to do," said Gracie, "to become a sort of Christian Mars."

"O, but St. Mark was just as useful in peace," said Vernon. "I'll tell you a story if you like. It's a well-known legend of Venice, and is called

The Demon Ship.

"In the year 1341 there was a great inundation. The waters of the Adriatic, rising at the furious impulse of a prolonged and terrible storm, raged about the city, overflowing the basements of the houses, and sweeping over the Piazza of St. Mark's till the billows of the sea broke against the Ducal Palace, and the Tower of St. Mark's, and the Cathedral. Panic seized upon the city. The terror was universal. The horrified people thronged to implore the aid of their patron saint, and the clergy with the people standing deep in the water, which was now all over the Cathedral floor, sent up petitions to invoke the interposition of Heaven.

"It was on a night when the storm and the greatest terror were at their height, that a poor fisherman, who was in his boat, at the bank of the Piazza, was accosted by a stranger, who had waded through the darkness towards him. This stranger wished to be taken to San Giorgio Maggiore. On the refusal of the fisherman, the other persisted, and offered to give him a large sum for his services. The fisherman was poor, and had never in all his life had such a chance of gaining so large a sum; yet the offer would not have tempted him to go. But there was something about the stranger which filled the fisherman with awe, and seemed to take away from him the power of refusal. Under this influence he prepared to obey, and taking his oars in silence, he put forth with the feeling of one who is going to certain death, and who has no power to fly.

"The storm was fierce, and even in the shelter of the city the sea ran high; and the fisherman, after rowing some distance, began to think that his awful companion had some protective power. At length the boat reached its destination, and there stood a figure as if waiting for them. This one got on board, and the fisherman felt for him something of the same awe which the first passenger had inspired.

"He was now ordered to row out to the mouth of the harbor. This time he did not dare to refuse; and besides, the very awe which kept him silent was associated with a conviction that his mysterious companions had power to save him from danger. And so, with this mixture of awe and confidence, he put forth all his efforts. At every moment the waves grew higher and more threatening. Never before had the fisherman known such a storm, and under ordinary circumstances it could not have lived in such a sea; but now the boat breasted the stormy waves right gallantly, and at length reached the mouth of the harbor without having shipped a drop of water from all those angry waves.

"Here the sea was terrific, and the storm raged worse than ever, at every moment rising to fresh fury and growing to a hurricane. But all the rage of the waves and the wrath of the storm was un-noticed by the fisherman in the presence of another spectacle which appeared before his eyes.

"For here, as he looked forth, he saw a huge galley driving down straight towards him, as though seeking to enter the city. But it was no ship in distress seeking a port, no ship of mortal man, that thus drove down before the gale. The strange ship was as black as midnight, with blue sulphur-ous flames disclosing her outlines and also her terrific crew. For the crew were all demons, who swarmed all over her masts and rigging, looking forth with furious eyes, gesticulating like maniacs, and howling and shrieking out words and impreca-tions that made his blood curdle within his veins, and his hair bristle with horror. Amid the din and uproar he could distinguish the words, over and over repeated with hideous curses — 'Up with the storm and sea! Down with Venice! Sink her in the waters!'

"At this moment his companions rose, making the sign of the cross, and the first passenger, in a stern voice of command, bade the demons to vanish.

"Scarce had the words been uttered than there was an instantaneous change. A wild and dreadful shriek rang out through the sky, the demon ship all seemed to collapse and tumble in upon itself, and vanished away utterly. The sea grew calm, the wind ceased, and deep silence reigned all around, while from afar there came to the ears of the astonished fisherman the sweet sounds of the bells of St. Mark's.

"At a sign from the elder of the passengers the fisherman now rowed back to San Giorgio, where the two got out.

"'Go to the governor,' said the first passenger, 'and tell him that but for us Venice would have been destroyed. I am St. Mark. My companion is St. George.' Then, taking a ring from his finger, he added, 'Show them this, and tell them to look for it in my treasury, whence it will be found missing.'

"The fisherman did as he was told. On examination the ring was found missing, and the fisherman's story was believed. They gave him a handsome reward and an annual pension. In addition to this, solemn services were instituted in honor of the saints who had interposed to save Venice from so direful a calamity."

"Well," said Gracie, "if a city does have a patron saint, it seems to me that fighting off demon ships is more in accordance with his Christian character than subduing foreign countries ; and so I'm much obliged to you for your story."

Vernon now took them to a place where there was a diamond-shaped slab of polished porphyry set in the pavement.

" This," said he, " is the place where the Emperor Frederic Barbarossa knelt when he made his submission to the pope."

" You will have to tell me all about it," said Gracie," for I'm sorry to say that I know absolutely nothing about the Emperor Frederic Barbarossa."

" I'll try and make the story as short as possible," said Vernon, " so as not to be tiresome."

And with this he proceeded to tell the story of

The Great Barbarossa.

" The war between Pope Alexander and the Emperor Frederic Barbarossa had been raging for seventeen years. At length the emperor had lost his power on the sea, and the time soon came when he was to lose it on the land. The league of the Lombard cities had proved thus far invincible, and now stood before him with a great army to fight the last battle for their liberties. Frederic hastened against them with a greater army, and the two opposing forces met at Legnano, where they fought one of the greatest battles of modern times. But Frederic had traitors in his camp, and Guelph, who led one quarter of his forces, held back from the contest. Frederic was defeated. His army was ruined, and he who had in the morning been the mightest ruler in Europe, in the evening fled from the field, with the prospect of irremediable ruin lowering all around him.

" His grand army was lost. Guelph was false. The followers of Guelph were preparing to stir up all Germany against him. In the days of his power he had scoffed at the curse of the pope: but now that he was a fallen man, the anathema crushed him into the dust. Never again could he hope to rise until that was taken away.

" Besides this, he thirsted for vengeance on the traitor to whom he attributed his ruin. For the sake of this he determined to sacrifice his pride. To get rid of the ban of the church — the terrible curse — was his first and most pressing necessity. Upon this he resolved, and he resolved also to submit even to the lowest humiliation if he might but accomplish this.

" Once before a Roman emperor had humbled himself before a pope, and had shown to the world that the invisible weapons of the church were far stronger than arms of steel or disciplined legions of valiant warriors. The world was now to learn this lesson a second time. The Emperor Henry IV. had humbled himself before Gregory VII. at Canossa ; and now Frederic Barbarossa went to repeat this act of self-abasement before Alexander at Venice.

"Venice heard and was glad. It was considered a triumph for the proud and valiant republic. The glory was Alexander's, but Venice would share that glory. She had already humbled the emperor at sea. She could share in the triumph of those who had humbled him at Legnano. She had helped the pope with her powerful arm in the days of his exile; she would now take a part in his triumph. The emperor was to bow down before the pope, but he was to do this act in Venice, and Venice should look on, and see it, and be glad.

"The emperor landed at the Piazzetta. The doge and all the nobility were there to receive him —an imposing cortége, representing all that was great or illustrious in Venice. In this way he was received, and then was conducted to the Piazza.

"There, on a chair in front of St. Mark's, sat the pope, his mighty antagonist,—mighty, yet poor — the man who had fought with him so long, and who had won at last. He was clad in his pontifical vestments, with the triple crown upon his head, while around him stood a brilliant assemblage of cardinals, archbishops, bishops, and other high ec- clesiastics. All stood except the pope. He alone was seated, and he waited with a calm and tranquil face for the emperor.

"The emperor came forward. Then he uncov- ered and prostrated himself, casting aside at the same time his purple mantle. Then he kissed the foot of the pope.

"And so there lay prostrate the mighty Frederic Barbarossa, Holy Roman Emperor, Lord of Germany and Italy, who claimed to be first monarch on earth. As he lay there thus prostrate, all the past came before the mind of Alexander. He had fought long and bravely. He had known the lowest depths of misfortune. He had known want and exile. He had been insulted, and persecuted, and hunted down over all Italy, by land and sea. He had known what it was to be alone, with nothing to rely on but his own inflexible soul. Now, at last, he had reached the hour of his triumph, and of that triumph he was not willing to lose one jot or tittle. He would enjoy it to the uttermost by abasing Federic to the uttermost.

"He placed his foot upon the head of the prostrate emperor, and said these words of Scripture :—

" 'Thou shalt tread upon the lion and the adder ; the young lion and the dragon shalt thou trample under foot.'

"From this bitter insult Frederic's soul revolted.

" 'It is not to *you*,' said he, in an indignant voice —'it is not to *you* that I bow ; it is to *St. Peter*.'

"Upon this the pope placed his foot a second time, and more firmly, upon the emperor's head.

" 'It is both to *me* and St. Peter,' he said.

"With this he was satisfied, and after this the reconciliation was effected, and the anathema was taken off, and the emperor restored to communion with the church amid the most magnificent ceremonies."

It was now too late in the day to visit the Ducal Palace ; so, after walking about the Piazza for a while, they returned to the gondola, and went up and down the Grand Canal. Venice appeared more beautiful and more picturesque than ever. Crowds of boats were out, and murmurs of conversation came over the water, mingled with the voice of song and the sharp cry of the gondoliers. Then came sunset, and our party returned to Vernon's house.

After dinner, Vernon set himself to the pleasing task of amusing his guests, in which there was not the slightest difficulty, for they all were in the highest possible spirits.

Clive and David were loud in their expressions of delight. Never had they seen any place which was equal to Venice. Naples, and Florence, and even Rome, were inferior.

"I'm very glad to hear that," said Gracie. "I've been half afraid, while I was enthusiastic about Venice, that you would crush me with your superior knowledge, and fling at my devoted head those very cities — Naples, and Florence, and Rome. And what makes it ever so much nicer is, that I feel so much at ease about poor dear auntie. I suppose I shall hear about her to-morrow—shan't I, Mr. Vernon?"

"Well, hardly to-morrow," said Vernon. "You see they will send their messenger to-morrow, and it is not likely that you will hear anything of her until the day after, unless she comes here."

"O, well," said Gracie, with a little sigh, "I shall leave it all to you and the police."

"The day after to-morrow," said Clive. "I suppose Uncle Moses will be here by that time."

"They'll be sorry enough," said David, "that they didn't come with us — won't they?"

"Won't they, though!" said Clive. "I bet they will."

Vernon was attentive to all his guests, but to Gracie he was most devoted. In fact, Gracie was one to whom every one felt inclined to devote himself, and David and Clive looked at her with that chivalrous homage which is felt by every high-minded boy for youth, and loveliness, and elegant refinement. All these were present in Gracie. She was like a sunbeam in the artist's home; her name was appropriate indeed, for there was an ineffable grace in her look, her attitude, her gestures, while in her voice there was a certain indefinable charm which was irresistible.

"He's awfully fond of Gracie," whispered Clive to David, as Vernon sat and talked with her.

"So am I," said David, with a low groan.

"You're not half so fond of her as I am," said Clive.

"Pooh!" said David; "you don't begin even to understand what it is to feel as I feel."

"I," said Clive, "I not understand! Let me tell you, mister —"

But here they were interrupted by Vernon.

" Come, boys," said he ; " I'm going to show some of my pictures: would you like to see them ? "

Wouldn't they, though !

The invitation was received with enthusiasm, and Vernon led the way to an adjoining apartment, which was fitted up as a studio. Here there was an easel with an unfinished picture. At one side of the room was another picture, and to this Vernon led them.

It represented a scene in a Venetian palace. There was a young man, thin and haggard, to whom an elderly lady was clinging. Opposite these sat an old man, richly dressed as a Venetian noble. He held a letter in his hands, which he appeared to be reading. The chief point in this picture was the old man's face. There was horror in it, and amazement, together with remorse ; and it seemed as if all these, struggling together, had quite overwhelmed him.

They all looked in profound silence, and Gracie at length asked what it was about.

" I will tell you afterwards," said Vernon ; " but before I tell you I should like to show you this picture. It is not quite finished, but you can see what the idea is."

This was the picture on the easel. It was a scene in a masquerade. They recognized the place, for it was the Grand Piazza. Amid the crowd there were three in masks. Two of these appeared to be lovers, who were shrinking back as if in fear; the third was a large, stern man, somewhat elderly, who was the chief figure. From behind his mask the artist had succeeded in suggesting an expression of intense rage and fury, which was stamped upon his cruel mouth, and gleamed from his fiery eyes.

"I wish we could know what these pictures are about," said Gracie.

"I have the stories written out," said Vernon, "and I'll read them to you, if you care to hear them. After that you can look at the pictures again, and let me know what you think of them."

They all returned to the room now, and Vernon, producing some manuscripts, began to read.

CHAPTER IV.

Vernon reads to his Guests the Story of Antenore and Galbajo.

ANTENORE was one of the haughtiest nobles of Venice. No one was so jealous as he about the rights and privileges of the patrician class, so obstinate in his refusal to grant any concessions to the lower orders, or so indignant at what he called their presumption, when any of them ventured by a fortunate speculation to increase his means, and rise a little in the scale of being. For there were many of these far beneath Antenore in rank, who had dared to make money, and to exhibit the signs of wealth in their persons and surroundings. With these he was compelled to have business connection, to traffic with them, to talk with them on the Piazza; but such intercourse was always revolting to his pride.

Among those who most particularly excited his dislike was the merchant Galbajo. His wealth was great; he had made it all himself; and yet he showed none of that vanity and self-assertion which often mark the self-made man. He was popular among the men of his own order, and his

simple and unaffected manners might have dis-
armed resentment everywhere. But Galbajo was
too prosperous: he had a genius for money-mak-
ing, and he could not remain free from the assaults
of envy and detraction. For this man of the people presumed to be fortunate when others were
unfortunate : in boldness of speculation, and in extent of enterprise, he began to rival the great
merchant princes themselves; and his uniform
success was such that Antenore darkly hinted at
mysterious violations of the law. The truth was,
that Galbajo had an unusual talent for commercial
enterprises; he was daring, yet prudent; watch-
ful, yet bold : moreover his household was simple,
and his personal expenditure small, so that all his
gains were kept to accumulate in his hands; while
the wealthy nobles, who lived in great state, expended their money as fast as they made it. All
this excited jealousy. Antenore's malicious hints
stirred up suspicion, and large numbers of people
were influenced by him to look upon Galbajo as a
successful knave and hypocrite, who under a pretence of great simplicity concealed a long career
of duplicity and crime.

Such was the state of affairs, when one day a
ship arrived from Smyrna for Galbajo. It was
just the time when the truce with the Turks had
ended, and war had recommenced. All other
merchants had recalled their ships. These ships
were in the docks, and the merchants were idle,

without much hope of resuming active enterprises. At such a time as this the arrival of Galbajo's ship excited universal comment, and Antenore intensified the suspicions that were expressed. Who was Galbajo, that he could do business when all other merchants are idle? How does it happen that he alone is not affected by the war? There must be some reason for this; and the reason is, that he has a secret and treasonable understanding with the enemy. Such were Antenore's words, and these sentiments were soon so wide-spread that the government took it up, and Galbajo was arrested.

The explanation which he gave to his judges was simple and straightforward. According to this, his ship had left Smyrna before the outbreak of the war, but had met with various unavoidable delays. A tempest had forced her to take refuge in Corfu, where she had been overhauled, and received repairs. This would account for the arrival of the ship from a Turkish port in time of war.

This simple explanation, however, was not received. The influence of Antenore was strong, and his dark suggestions were listened to only too readily. Galbajo's statement was taken to be the cunning invention of one who had prepared himself for the possibility of discovery, and had armed himself against it. It was plausible, but the accusation was more probable. It was more likely that Galbajo should be successful as a rogue than as an honest man. The result was, that Galbajo was found guilty. The sentence was a severe one. He was condemned for plotting treason against the state. The ordinary punishment was death; but, as there was some flaw in the evidence, the judges gave him the benefit of the doubt, and were willing to consider the charge as not exactly proved. His life would therefore be spared, and the state would be satisfied with banishing him for life. At the same time one half of his property was to be confiscated.

The confiscation of one half of Galbajo's property meant the loss of nearly all, for it was disposed of by a forced sale, and in time of war, too, so that it was virtually sacrificed. Then, after the loss of all, the unfortunate Galbajo found before him a still greater loss — that of his country. His sentence was banishment for life, and with the wreck of his property he prepared to leave. He knew well who it was that had been at the bottom of all his misfortunes. Antenore never had taken any pains to conceal his hate, and Galbajo had heard of all his words and acts. But opposition was useless, and resistance impossible; so he submitted without a word, and left the unjust city to go in his old age on a far distant exile.

The war now went on. The Turks were triumphant everywhere. The Venetian fleets were driven from the sea, and the Crescent flag waved proudly where once had floated the haughty Lion

of St. Mark. Defeat followed defeat. The Venetians sank into despondency. At length all these
misfortunes culminated in the tidings which came
one day — that the last fleet of the republic had
been worsted in a great naval action; that it had
fled in disgrace, with the loss of half its ships;
that thousands of Venetians had been made prisoners; and that the command of the seas was lost forever. With the general distress we have nothing
to do. It is enough to add, that among those who
were captured by the Turks was the only son of
Antenore.

To that unhappy noble this blow was a crushing
one. All the hopes of his family had been centred
upon this young man; for he was the only son, and
the last prop of an ancient house. To him, and to
him alone, the father looked as his successor to the
proud honors of the Antenori, and as the stay and
solace of his declining years. Now he was gone,
and with him the family name and family fame
would sink into oblivion.

There was no hope whatever to Antenore. It
was not then as it is now, in this nineteenth century, when civilized nations are at war, and efforts
are made to alleviate its inevitable horrors; when
the prisoners are treated with humanity, and have
hopes of speedy exchange. War in this age was
very different, and especially so when it was war
between Turks and Christians. In one sense
there was always war with the Turks. The Mo-

hammedans would never consent to make peace.
They always called it a truce, and made it for a
stipulated term of years, but always merely for their
own convenience. During these times of truce,
there was often an exchange of prisoners, and also
a chance for ransoming Christian captives, if they
could only be found. But now all chance of exchange or ransom was far, far away, for the war
had only begun. Years must pass before it could
be ended; and who could say whether Venice herself might survive until then. All those years the
captive must languish. The thought was anguish
to Antenore. Willingly would he have given his
own life to redeem that beloved son from captivity.
Such a fate was worse than death. For death,
with all its horror, once past, might be endured,
and the bereaved ones might be soothed by time;
but captivity forced itself forever on the thoughts;
and the wretched father bore with him always the
image of his son, pining in chains, fainting under
the scourge, or dying daily of a broken heart.

The Palazzo Antenore was shrouded in gloom.
All joy was banished. The stricken mother sank
under this blow, and could only wish for death.
The father tried to bear it with a Stoic's pride;
but pride was only a poor support when mental
anguish was undermining all the foundations of
life. Yet still he struggled as well as he could
against his deep affliction, and tried to find in the
routine duties of his official station some means of
distracting his thoughts.

At length, one day there came a galley to
Venice. A young man disembarked, and, taking
a gondola, proceeded to the Palazzo Antenore.
The vast pile looked gloomy and deserted. A
few servants stood in the hall with dreary and
dejected looks. No longer were there those gay
throngs which of old had filled the great house
with life and animation. All was desolation and
melancholy.

The young man rushed in. The servants stared
in amazement. He dashed by them without a
word, ascending the grand staircase, and travers-
ing the great gallery, whose walls were covered
with pictures, until at length he reached a room at
the end. This he entered.

There was but one occupant in the room — an
old man, who sat with his head bowed in his
hands. So absorbed was he in his thoughts that
he neither saw nor heard the new comer. The
young man stood for a moment, and then went up
to him.

" Father !

It was but a single word. At the sound of that
word, and of that voice, the old man started to his
feet, and stared at the new comer with a white face,
and something like horror in his look.

" O, my son !" he moaned ; " O, my son ! Is it all
over ? Do you come from the dead to tell — !"

" The dead !" cried the other, catching the old
man in his embrace. " No, thank God ! I am alive.

I have just arrived, and have hurried here to bring you the good news."

The old man trembled, but it was with excess of utter joy. He could not say one word; but holding his beloved son in his arms, he clung to him, and sobbed convulsively.

"My mother," said the young man, "how is she? Is she — is she alive?"

"Yes," said Antenore. "O, yes, come — come and raise her up from her despair. Come and show her that her son yet lives. But no — wait — not yet — the shock will be too much. Let me go first, and prepare her. Wait."

He retired hastily, and after a few moments' absence returned. Another was with him, wild with joy. It was the mother, who had read the wonderful news in her husband's face, and without waiting for any words, had hurried forth to meet her son.

That meeting cannot be described. For a long time nothing was uttered except ejaculations expressive of every variation of love, wonder, and joy. But at last, as the first rush of feeling began to subside, they were eager to know how he had escaped, or whether he had been a captive at all.

"A captive!" said the young man. "Ay, that I have been, and I have tasted all the utmost bitterness of such a lot. But Heaven had pity on me, and sent to me, in my misery, the noblest of men. He saved me."

"Saved you? What!" cried Antenore. "Is

there any living man who has done this thing? O
that I could see him! Is he here? Did he come
with you? Why did you not bring him with you?
O that I could see him! If he is poor, I would
share with him all that I have in the world; if he
is rich, I would seek to keep him here with me:
and in either case, I would fall on my knees before
him, and tell him that I thanked him as I thank
my God."

"He did not come with me," said the son; "he
is a Greek. He is rich also, and needs no reward.
God alone can reward him; we never can. His
name is Angelus."

"Angelus! Rightly is he called Angelus,"
cried Antenore, "for he has been an angel, sent
by Heaven to restore my son. Is he indeed a
mortal man? A Greek! Impossible. Are you sure
that he is a mortal man?"

"He is a man," said the son, "yet the noblest
of men. He saw me languishing, sick, broken-
hearted, dying. He purchased me. He took me
to his home. He nursed me, and brought me back
to life and health. Never did any one man show
such love to another. It was as though my own
father had found me, and had saved me. And I
loved him as a son, for I saw that he loved me as
a father. O, father! O, mother! pray while you
live for the noble Angelus, who saved me from
my agony. And he, too, had his sorrows. I could
see that he was a man of woe — a man who had

suffered some great bereavement. It seemed to me always as if he had lost an only son, and that I reminded him of that son, and therefore he loved me."

The aged parents sat close by their son, each holding a hand. There seemed to them something inexpressibly sad in this description of Angelus — the one who had lost an only son. Tears came to their eyes: they pressed more closely the hands of that dear one who had been lost, but restored.

"It was his very love for me," continued the son, "which sent me home. Had his love been less, he might have kept me, and merely sent word to you of my safety: but he loved me so well that he sacrificed even his own feelings; and I know this, for he told me so himself. 'Your father,' said he to me, 'does not love you better than I. It is because I love you so well, that I can bear to give you up. I shall be happier in your happiness than in my own. I shall miss you; but I shall always console myself that you are happy with your parents, and in your dear native land.'"

"Did he say that?" said Antenore, in a faltering voice. "Did he say that? Then, O, my son, I can find it in my heart to wish that you had staid with him longer, and merely sent me word of your safety."

"I proposed this," said the son, "but he would not consent. 'No,' said he: 'go home. Your parents are old. Go now, or you may never see them again;' and so I left him."

"O, may the Lord of mercy bless the man who showed such love and mercy to my son!"

Such was the ejaculation of Antenore at the conclusion of his son's story.

"He gave me a letter," said the son, "for you."

"A letter! for me!" said Antenore. "O, let me see it."

The son drew forth a letter from his pocket, and handed it to his father. Antenore drew off a little, and with a face of eager and joyous anticipation, broke the seal. He read the following: —

"With this letter you will receive back to your heart your only son, the last of your line. It is not because he is an Antenore that I have helped him, but because I was won, in spite of myself, by his face, by his looks, and by the tones of his voice; for they all brought back before me my beloved, my lost Venice. Banished by you, I came to Alexandria, and live here in disguise as a Greek: but my heart clings to my country, and for me there is nothing but misery in exile. I have wealth and comforts, but these are nothing. I met your son by chance, and I loved him as my own son, for he was a Venetian. Willingly would I have kept him with me to soothe my exile, but I loved him too well for that, and so I send him home. Take him, then, for you are his father; take him — a gift from the man you most hate; take him from the man whom you never expected to find your benefactor; for know, O Antenore, that the deliverer of your only son from slavery is — the banished   GALBAJO."

Antenore dropped the letter from his trembling hands. His face lost that flush of joy which his son's return had brought, and was now livid with horror. He could only gasp one word, and that was, —

" *Galbajo!* "

He was overwhelmed now with remorse and bitter self-reproach. Now he learned, when too late, the true character of that man whose noble heart had been well nigh broken by the torments which had been inflicted upon him. And why? For no other cause than a cursed jealousy. And this was his return. His joy at the sight of his son was marred by this remorse, and he felt that he could never know peace of mind again until he should see Galbajo in Venice.

To this work he now devoted himself. He was successful. Antenore's explanations, and his story of Galbajo's noble conduct, together with the influence which he had in high quarters, led to measures which ended in an order for the termination of the period of banishment. A Turkish prisoner was found, who was released in order to convey to Alexandria the welcome news. Galbajo received the letters sent him, and succeeded in effecting his escape. He at length returned to Venice, and there Antenore fulfilled the promise that he had made in the first meeting with his son ; all the fervent gratitude to his son's benefactor, which he had then expressed, was now plainly manifested : and the old jealous hatred gave way to respectful affection and intimate friendship.

5

CHAPTER V.

*The second Story. — The wonderful Adventures of
Soranzo.*

T was a great festival at St. Mark's. The interior of the gorgeous church was filled with
a devout multitude. The altars were all
ablaze with lights, which flashed upon the polished
marbles and the gilded domes. The smoke of in-
cense rolled on high ; the peal of the organ came
reverberating along the arches : and the antipho-
nal chant of the choristers mingled with the intoning
of the priests, or the miserere of five thousand worshippers.

One young man there was in that great crowd
who did not seem to be joining in the common
worship. The object of his worship was not " Our
Lady," but nevertheless it was a lady of slender
and graceful figure, who was kneeling with droop-
ing head upon the stone pavement not far away.
He, too, was kneeling, yet in such a way that he
could look at her; and his eyes never removed
themselves from her. It was a face of exquisite
beauty, of classic features, with that creamy white
complexion which is so rarely found, and which

was long the boast of Venetians as the chief charm of their women. The head was bent forward, the downcast eyes sought the pavement, and the long, silken fringe of eyelashes hid them from sight. As the young man gazed, she raised herself and looked full towards him. Their eyes met; a slight flush passed over her face, a quick smile over her lips. It was a recognition, but it was only of a moment's duration, for her eyes once more fell, and she did not raise them again.

At length the service was over, and the crowd began to disperse. The young lady walked away along with an elderly woman, her attendant. The young man followed close, and in the crowd succeeded in slipping a letter into the lady's hand, which letter was taken by the other as naturally as though she had expected it. Then she passed away.

Bianca Polani, the young lady just mentioned, belonged to one of the greatest families in Venice. Her father had won distinction at home and abroad, and was noted for his insatiable ambition. To rise higher and higher had always been his aim: to those above him he was obsequious, to those below him tyrannical; and if he loved his beautiful daughter, it was rather because he saw in her the means of making some lofty alliance by which he might gain additional rank or power. From such a man the lady Bianca's lover, Soranzo, could never hope to receive any favors whatever. Nothing was against Soranzo but his poverty: yet this, in Venice, was a dire offence. It was always a purse-proud community — an aristocracy of merchant princes, who prided themselves on their lineage, it is true, yet always allowed the genealogical tree to be influenced by the ledger. Soranzo's family was of great renown. His name was inscribed on the Libro d' Oro, the Golden Book, which contained the names of the Venetian nobles. Doges had been chosen in former ages out of that illustrious line. Their very downfall had been glorious. It was during the war of Chiozza. The Soranzi had given up everything that they possessed in the hour of their country's direst need, and after the struggle was over, nothing was left but the walls of their ancestral palace. True, the state had endeavored to reward all those who had done it service, but its rewards were chiefly in rank and honors. The wealth of the Soranzi never came back. Nothing was left but their glorious past: and Giuglio Soranzo entered upon life, the owner of a splendid name, and an empty palace, which was going to ruin from its very vastness. He had seen Bianca, and loved her. His love was returned. They had met and told their mutual love. But their meetings had to be clandestine, for the poor Soranzo could not be admitted to pay his attentions to the daughter of the wealthy Polani.

On this occasion, Soranzo had given Bianca a note which imparted very important intelligence.

For the young man, full of energy and hope, could no longer live in idleness at Venice. His very desire to win Bianca prompted him to be up and doing. He had, therefore, offered his services to the government. His offer had been accepted, and the letter informed Bianca of his speedy departure. It also implored her to grant him a final meeting on the following evening. There was to be a masquerade on the Piazza. He would expect her.

So beautiful and wealthy a maiden as Bianca was not without crowds of suitors, but among them all by far the most distinguished was Malapieri. He was about as old as Bianca's father, — a noble of immense wealth and great distinction. He had lost his first wife, and was anxious to place the beautiful Bianca over his household. To Polani this proposal was most acceptable. An alliance with Malapieri would give him that additional strength which he desired, in order to advance himself in the state ; and therefore, so far as he could act in the matter, the affair was decided. Far different, however, was it with Bianca. Apart from her love of Soranzo, she could never have consented to become the wife of Malapieri. He was old, and harsh, and abhorrent. She both hated and feared him. To pass her life with such a man would be terrible. Her family, however, treated her repugnance with indifference. They set it down as a young girl's whims. At the same time they suspected that she might have some love affair. These suspicions were communicated to Malapieri, and Bianca became closely watched.

Bianca, however, had one faithful friend. This was the old attendant already mentioned. She had taken care of Bianca all her life, and knew all her secrets, not excepting even this. It was by her connivance that Soranzo had been able to speak to his love, and with her assistance Bianca expected to see him again.

The masquerade took place. Bianca went there with her attendant, wearing a dress which Soranzo knew, and she was at once accosted by her lover.

"I cannot live without you," said he; "and therefore I am going to leave you."

"To leave me!" she repeated, mournfully.

"Yes; that is my only hope. I wish to win distinction, and wealth also. I have got a post in the fleet that is going to Negropont."

"Negropont?"

Bianca could say nothing; she could only repeat these words, which seemed to her full of despair.

"It is best," said Soranzo. "I shall have a chance to distinguish myself. Trust me; when I come back, I shall no longer be obliged to stand outside your door."

Other words followed, in the midst of which Bianca suddenly caught Soranzo's arm with a convulsive grasp.

"He knew us!" she murmured.

"He ? Who ?"

Bianca looked towards a man who had just passed.

"It is Malapieri!" she said, in a frightened voice.
"I know his dress. He stared at us so fiercely
that his eyes were like coals of fire. He must be
watching us."

Soranzo knew very well what Malapieri's attentions were; and he thought it quite probable that
the aged lover was jealous.

"O, never mind," said he. "That danger is removed. For Malapieri is to command the fleet,
and so he will not trouble you till he returns."

"Malapieri!" cried Bianca, in consternation;
"and you!—are you going with him?"

"O, yes. Malapieri's appointment was very sudden. He did not like it, but could not get out of
it. It came in a very flattering way, although I
dare say there are some who would be very well
pleased if he never came back."

"I know one person," said Bianca, with a little
sigh.

Their interview soon ended. Like others, it was
very short, and soon the two lovers had bidden each
other a long farewell.

The forebodings which Bianca had felt as to Soranzo's sailing under Malapieri were soon proved
to be well founded The position of Malapieri gave
him absolute power over all in the fleet; all felt his
severity; but most of all, Soranzo. He had discovered that this youth was the object of Bianca's

favor, without whom the young maiden might perhaps have been won by himself, without a father's coercion. Malapieri was therefore full of jealous fury, and set himself on the watch to gratify his passion by the ruin of his rival. The task was not a difficult one. Words of bitter insult which he addressed to Soranzo were resented somewhat warmly, whereupon the young man was at once arrested and put in irons. It was a wanton exercise of authority, and an unlawful act, for no Venetian noble could be put in irons except by the Council of Ten. But Malapieri was resolved to take the consequences, and felt confident in being able to hold his own against the friendless youth.

On reaching the mouth of the Adriatic Sea, a Turkish fleet appeared. It was not superior in numbers to that of Malapieri, but nevertheless the Venetian admiral resolved to avoid an engagement. The government, he said, had sent him to take supplies to Negropont, and a sea fight, even if successful, might ruin the purpose of the expedition. He therefore steered in another direction, and the Turkish fleet set forth in pursuit. Now, when Soranzo had been thrown in irons, he had been transferred to one of the galleys, which was the smallest and slowest in the fleet. As the chase went on, this galley fell behind the others. Her captain signalled, but in vain. Malapieri paid no attention to the signals, but urging on the rest of the fleet to the utmost, fled at full speed. The

Turks, meanwhile, pursued with equal vigor, and soon overhauled Soranzo's galley. In an instant it was boarded and captured, and all were made prisoners. After this the Turks kept up the pursuit for some time, but without gaining on the fugitives, until at last, as evening came, the Turkish admiral signalled to return.

So ended the bright hopes of Soranzo. Stopped short before he had a chance to strike a single blow; instead of renown, captivity; instead of Bianca, a brutal Turkish master: he might well have sunk into despair. The faint hope remained of being captured by a Venetian fleet, but even this died out, and he found himself at last landed at Smyrna, where he was handed over with some others to a Turkish aga, who lived at Vourla, a seaport near by.

Malapieri succeeded in reaching Negropont; but here a series of disasters befell him. The Venetians were beset by the Turks. Post after post fell into the hands of the enemy. The island proved untenable. It was lost to Venice, and at length the unfortunate admiral returned in a single miserable galley, leaving the rest of his fleet in the hands of the Turks, or at the bottom of the sea. His arrival caused consternation in Venice. It seemed ominous of the future. The dreaded Turk was sweeping away from Venice, one by one, those possessions for which she had expended so much blood and treasure. The Christian capital of the East had fallen. The Morea was lost. Candia was threatened. Venice was insulted in her own waters, and the espousal of the Adriatic was fast growing a miserable mockery The Crescent was driving out the Cross: the Mediterranean was growing a Turkish lake ; and soon the fierce sultan would be sending his navies to attack Venice itself. Such was the universal feeling: and if Malapieri escaped blame, it was because all men, in their dejection, attributed his failure to the general ill fortune which had come upon Venice.

Malapieri now returned to his palace, glad that he had saved his own precious life, and eager now to carry through the important project of marrying Bianca. He would make amends for his misfortunes abroad by seeking after happiness at home, and successful love should requite him for unsuccessful ambition.

Meanwhile Bianca had heard all ; she had heard that Soranzo had been mutinous, had been arrested, and had been captured by the Turks. Malapieri himself told her his own story, and added that it was fortunate that Soranzo had been captured, for if he had been brought back to Venice he would have been executed. This speech only increased Bianca's hate towards Malapieri: yet at the same time the thought of her lover's hopeless captivity preyed upon her heart. She lost all taste for pleasure, shut herself up, and rapidly grew ill. The physician came to see her, but could do nothing. In fact, Bianca's wretchedness was far beyond the skill of any physician. Her father saw it all with deep concern. Her mother understood the cause, and said that her heart was broken. And so for a while they forbore to say anything about Malapieri.

But Malapieri was impatient. He was advanced in years. Bianca, he said, could afford to wait, but he couldn't. Better to marry now, and no doubt under his tender care she would soon grow better. Old Polani was won over by this, and began to insist on Bianca's marriage. He himself made a set speech to her, in which he spoke solemnly of the necessity of children obeying their parents. To all of this Bianca said not one word, but afterwards, as she lay weeping on her mother's bosom, she sobbed out, " I shall die; drive me from you if you choose ; but at least you might let me die at home, and not among strangers whom I hate."

" O, no," said her mother, who tried to console her, though it was with tearful eyes and quaking heart. " O, no, dearest child ; you will live to be the first lady in Venice — perhaps the dogaressa."

While Bianca was thus mourning and weeping, Soranzo was far away in Vourla, a slave, laboring with other slaves about the estate of his master. But his ardent and impetuous nature never for one moment submitted to his fate ; on the contrary, he always looked out with sleepless vigilance to see if there were any chances of escape.

There were other Christian captives here, and a Turkish guard was considered sufficient to prevent any attempt at escape, so that they were not bound. With these, Soranzo discussed the chances of flight, and soon proposed to them a daring plan. Out in the little harbor was a galley, which was used by the aga for certain duties to which he was appointed. There were two hundred Christian slaves on board at the oars, with a small guard of Turkish marines. The plan of Soranzo was to take advantage of the moment when the Turks were at prayer, attack them, disarm them, seize the galley, and fly.

It was a bold plan, and was crowned with complete success. The Turks were overpowered, their arms were seized, and a rush was then made upon the galley. The marines here fired a few shots without effect, and then in a panic leaped into the sea. Soranzo, in a few fierce words, told the Christian rowers what had happened, and bade them row for their lives if they hoped ever again to see their country and their friends. The rowers understood the whole, and rowed as they had never done before. The galley stood out to sea, several Turkish ships of war were passed, but no pursuit was made, for the galley was supposed to be on duty.

On the following day they were far out at sea. Here they fell in with a Turkish galley. Soranzo's rowers were exhausted; to fly was impossible; to fight was equally so, for the supply of arms was inadequate. For a moment it seemed as though all was lost, but before long his inventive genius, stimulated by the desperate peril around him, contrived a plan of attack. Sending men aloft, he loosened the fastenings of the long yard by which it was bound to the mast, and also unfurled the immense sail. The sail caught the wind; Soranzo stood at the helm, and directing the men to row with all their might, bore down full upon the Turkish galley. The Turks, unprepared for this sudden attack, hauled round so as to rake Soranzo's vessel with a volley of all sorts of missiles. Soranzo received the volley, but without much harm, and still drove on. The Turks prepared to board. Soranzo's galley struck the enemy's quarter, and as they were all crowded together there, so as to board, the immense yard, with its sail loosened from its fastenings by the shock of the collision, fell upon them, entangling and half smothering them in its folds; so that Soranzo and his men, who poured on board, captured them all without resistance.

The prize was a great one. Five hundred Christians were at the oars. These were freed at once. Two hundred Turks laid down their arms. These were distributed among the rescued Christians. What was better, great stores of weapons were found, sufficient to arm all the Christians in both ships, so that they now felt themselves equal to encounter any Turkish force. Finally, the Turkish prisoners were consigned to the oars, and forced to row the galleys. The number, however, was not quite sufficient, so that the Christians were intermingled with them.

They now resumed their journey. For three days nothing happened, but on the fourth they encountered three Turkish ships. Soranzo was bent upon an encounter. In a fiery harangue he poured his own spirit into his followers. " Let us not go back home empty-handed," he cried. " Let us revenge ourselves on these devils for all our wrongs. Those ships must be ours, or I will not survive the fight."

The men responded with a wild cheer. Up went the standard of Venice to the mast-head, displaying the proud blazonry of the Winged Lion of St. Mark, and Soranzo bore down upon the enemy.

He had now thought upon another manœuvre, and had instructed his men to carry it out. The first galley was to engage the smallest of the Turks, board her, and carry her by force of superior numbers, and while fighting, free the Christian oarsmen. He himself determined to engage the other two.

He now caused all the heaviest weights on board to be placed on one side. On a given signal the men were to rush to that side so as to bear down the galley, and then make an attack upon the Turks from that direction. With this plan he drove upon the enemy, and soon had closed with them. He steered so as to bring his galley between two of the largest ; and then, just as he reached them, he gave the word of command. In an instant several hundred men sprang to the port side of the galley, and bore it down deep in the water; at the same instant all the oars on the starboard side were raised high, and formed a palisade through which the Turks on the ship on that side could not pass. At the same time, the Turkish galley on the port side, which had drawn up close so as to board, was secured with grappling-irons, and the Christians flung themselves aboard of her. They freed the Christian rowers, and armed them. The struggle was fierce, but the Turks were altogether outnumbered, and threw down their arms.

Meanwhile the starboard Turkish ship, bewildered by this unheard-of manœuvre, tried to board Soranzo's galley, and drew in closer, just as the men were assailing the ship on the port side. The sudden departure of such a body of men caused Soranzo's galley to sink back to her former position, in doing which, the oars of the starboard galley were drawn down under her bottom, and all entangled and broken, while Soranzo's oars came down upon the heads of the Turks on her deck, filling them with confusion.

At this instant, Soranzo, with a shout, led the remainder of his men into the midst of the disordered Turks in the starboard galley. He was followed by crowds of the freed Christian rowers from the port galley. The Turks fought fiercely, but the Christians fought with the fury of tigers. The burning words of Soranzo rang in their ears, and stirred them to madness. They were fighting, not for life or liberty, but for revenge. They had been made captive, and exiled. They had been subjected to mockery, and blows, and insults, from wretched barbarians whom they despised; now was the hour for vengeance, when they could make a fit return for all that they had suffered. Again the Christian rowers in this galley were freed, and lent their aid in the strife. The Turks were everywhere outnumbered, yet still resisted, and rallied round the poop, where their commander, a huge Moor, cimeter in hand, hurled defiance at his enemies.

Towards this man Soranzo forced his way at the head of his bravest followers. As he came within reach, the huge Moor raised his cimeter. The next instant it descended like a flash; but Soranzo was a master of fence, and as the weapon fell it struck his uplifted rapier, and glided aside harmless, while, in a moment after, that rapier had pierced the heart of the Moor through and through.

At the fall of the Moor a cry of despair escaped the Turks. They threw down their arms. The Christians stopped in their career of victory. It was Soranzo's stern command.

"Kill no more!" he cried. "Put these prisoners at the oars. We want them all, for we must cut our way through other Turkish fleets before we reach home."

Meanwhile the other galley had been engaged in a fierce fight. But Soranzo's tactics had given the Christians the advantage. They had flung themselves on board the Turk, and had at once set free and armed the Christian rowers. The fight was on the deck of the Turkish galley, and was kept up obstinately until the fall of the Moor. Then these men, seeing the surrender of the others, likewise flung down their arms. The prisoners were now put at the oars, and the victorious Christians prepared to resume their voyage.

Upon looking around, Soranzo discovered, to his amazement, that the largest vessel was the very one which had been commanded by Malapieri. It had been captured at Negropont. From this, Soranzo, for the first time, knew that his enemy must have met with disaster. This discovery made his triumph seem all the sweeter.

And now the vestiges of the conflict were all effaced. Turks replaced Christians at the oars, while at the mast-head of the largest galley floated a Venetian flag, which Soranzo found on board. Expecting other fights, he kept in constant preparation, but his anticipations were not fulfilled. No more enemies appeared; and at length, far away on the northern horizon, the rejoicing Christians saw the lofty tower of St. Mark's.

Soranzo's fleet arrived at a time when no one

was expecting anything. There were marks of triumph, too, about the new comers which riveted the gaze of all. High in air floated the proud Lion of St. Mark's, with streamers dancing all around in the breeze, while from the stern of all the ships were trailed the Crescent flags of the Turks. Some of the ships had a Venetian look, others were evidently Turkish; yet these all formed part of some triumph which the Lion of St. Mark had won — a triumph most wonderful, most unaccountable, yet most sweet, since it came upon the heels of so many disasters. As the fleet drew nearer, it seemed as though the whole population had gone forth in boats. The water was covered with them. Those who first reached the galleys heard the news, and from them it passed to others, amplified and enlarged with the usual exaggerations. A great Turkish fleet had been destroyed; five thousand Christians had been freed: such were some of the rumors; yet among all, there was one name which was upon the lips of all, a name about which there could be no mistake; a name once illustrious in Venetian history, but never before associated with so splendid an achievement as this — the name of Soranzo!

Soranzo came back, and all Venice had already known how he had gone away. He had been dishonored by Malapieri — by that Malapieri who had delivered him up as a captive to the Turk, who had fled in terror from pursuers, who had lost a gallant fleet, and sacrificed the lives of a valiant host for nought. And here was his victim! With a great fleet the base Malapieri could do nothing; but Soranzo, out of his own valor, had won a new fleet for Venice!

Thus Soranzo came back with his name on the lips and in the hearts of all. It was a triumphant entry. As he landed at St. Mark's, it was with difficulty that his boat could reach the shore. On the Piazza it was with greater difficulty that he could pass. Parents saw in him the savior of their children; the hero who had snatched from captivity so many gallant souls; all saw in him one who was the savior of the state. He was overwhelmed by the throng. The air was rent with acclamations. The gallant band that followed him were beset and eagerly questioned; and many, overcome with emotion, fell upon their knees, and tried to kiss the hand of Soranzo. At last he succeeded in working his way through the crowd, and reached the Ducal Palace. Here, at the head of the Giant's Stairs, stood the doge, who had come forth to see with his own eyes the hero of this amazing and unexpected exploit, and also to exhibit the sympathy of the government with this outburst of patriotic emotion. To him Soranzo made his report, and handed over to him the jewelled turban and the cimeter of Noureddin — the Turkish Capitan Pasha — the terror of the Ægean Sea.

On that day there were two men who did not share the general joy.

One was Malapieri. At the return of Soranzo
in such a way his black and cruel heart quailed
with terror. No one knew so well as he the extent
of his own perfidy. Conscience made him cowardly. What if Soranzo, this popular hero, should
now denounce him! His own ears had heard words
of terror. The populace who cheered for Soranzo
also hurled imprecations at the name of Malapieri.
Against Soranzo poor and friendless it would have
been easy to struggle; but how could he hope to
contend with Soranzo the hero — and popular idol!
He looked far ahead. He judged of Soranzo by
himself, and saw himself the victim of a vengeful
enemy. It seemed as if all was lost. His only
safety lay in immediate flight. He did not linger,
but the very day that saw the triumph of Soranzo
saw the flight of Malapieri into an exile that terminated only with death.

The other uneasy spirit was Polani. He had
never injured Soranzo. He had only despised him
and slighted him. He had also sought to draw Bianca from him. He now feared lest Soranzo might
feel vengeful, and could only hope that he would
spare him for Bianca's sake. He determined to see
him at once in the hour of his triumph, to offer his
congratulations, and to try whether his love for Bianca had changed. As for Malapieri, he understood
well that the sun of that noble had set forever.

Thus the old Polani stood at the foot of the Giant's Stairs, waiting for an opportunity to speak to

Soranzo. At length the young man came forth, and descended the steps. He saw Polani at once, and with a flush of eager joy hurried towards him.

"Bianca!" he said.

The old man had been on the point of beginning a solemn congratulation, but he was shrewd enough to see that there was a far pleasanter subject. No — he had not forgotten — that eager look, those tremulous tones, showed that the stout heart which never quailed in battle was all quivering with anxious emotion at the thought of Bianca.

"She's well," said Polani, as he grasped Soranzo's hand in both of his. "She has been anxious about you. She saw your ships, and heard your name shouted out by the whole city. She has been waiting ever since to catch a glimpse of you."

All this was mere guess-work, yet it was perfectly true. Polani had conjectured well, and knew exactly what effect this would have on Bianca.

"Will you allow me to offer you my poor hospitality?" he continued; "we should like to hear how you escaped — and Bianca."

Soranzo pressed his hand fervently, and said not a word. Polani understood him, and they both turned to go.

It took about an hour to get through the crowd of men and boats, but at length they reached the Palazzo Polani.

It was all true. Bianca had heard all. In an

instant she had started up from her couch, where she had lain down to die of a broken heart, and had come back to vigorous life, and bounding hope, and exultant joy.

"He will be here!" she said to her mother. "He will be here! He is coming to me at last!"

And she was right. She knew her father's nature, and she knew Soranzo's love. As for Soranzo, the triumph of that day had all been as nothing compared with the deep, unutterable bliss which he felt as he entered the Palazzo Polani, and caught Bianca in his arms.

CHAPTER VI.

Poor Old Uncle Moses. — Deep Anxiety. — Pursuit of the Fugitives. — Bologna. — Ferrara. — Padua. — The Track lost. — Heroic Resolve of Uncle Moses. — On to Venice.

ET us now return to Uncle Moses and his doings. After taking leave of Clive and David, the unhappy uncle looked as though he had lost all that he most loved on earth. He returned to the hotel. Frank and Bob were away, intent upon their own amusements, and nothing was left for Uncle Moses but to brood over the troubles of his too anxious heart. Bitterly he regretted that he had given his consent to this separation. How could he know what might befall them? Away among strangers in a foreign land, without an uncle's care, it seemed to him that they were exposed to the most frightful perils. That they had a talent for getting into difficulties he knew but too well; and though thus far they had always got out of them again without harm, yet he had no assurance that this would always be so. Indeed, his fears all led him to expect the opposite, and to think that while David and Clive would still have their ill luck in falling into danger, they would lose their good luck in getting out.

When Frank and Bob returned, they were shocked to see the condition into which their beloved and revered relative had worked himself. He seemed utterly prostrated, and was so ill able to rouse himself that he could scarcely speak. At first they thought that he was ill, but they soon found that it was the mind that was affected, and not the body. Now, the departure of Clive and David had not made the smallest difference to Frank and Bob. They were usually accustomed to run in couples, and going to Bologna seemed no more to them than going to the other side of the Arno. But the anxiety and the deep distress of Uncle Moses was too serious a thing to be disregarded, and they perceived at once that they must sacrifice all their own tastes and plans to his comfort.

It was not long before Uncle Moses told them his whole mind. He told them that he could not endure another day of such anxiety as this; that he was anxious to go after Clive and David; to be with them, and have them all under his own eye; as for themselves, they could enjoy themselves quite as well in Bologna as in Florence; and that they must get ready to go on the following morning. This announcement, which was made with unusual decision, was received by the two without a word of objection.

"Certainly," said Frank. "It don't matter much to us, Uncle Mo. If you wish it, we shall be quite willing. At the same time you mustn't allow yourself to fret and worry so much about nothing. Why, if this goes on, you'll not be able to travel, and one of us will have to go and bring them back."

"Heaven forbid!" said Uncle Moses. "Don't you hint at sich a thing. Only you let me get to Bolony, an' you ain't going to catch me lettin' any of you out o' my sight agin."

The prospect of going on to Bologna and rejoining the lost boys was so grateful to Uncle Moses, that it rapidly restored him to something like his usual cheerfulness. He had been brooding all day long over his troubles, and now that he had made a clean breast of it, he felt unspeakably relieved. As for Frank and Bob, they felt quite rejoiced at the change in him, and comforted him with their assurances that they would meet Clive and David without fail.

"Unless, indeed," said Frank, "they have got so disgusted with Bologna as to come back here."

"That's an important idee," said Uncle Moses. "They might feel as bad as I did, and might be comin' back just as we were goin' on. I think I'd best write a short note of explanation, in case they should come back."

This gave Uncle Moses something to do, and he proceeded to write a letter explaining his departure, which he left with the concierge, to be given to Clive and David in the event of their return.

Now, there had been no very definite arrangement as to time. The boys had specified two or three days. Afterwards, as we know, they had acted on the supposition of an allowance of three days, and with this understanding they wrote their letter from Padua. As for Uncle Moses, he had not thought of any very definite time, and to leave on the next day did not seem to him likely to disarrange any plans whatever. Accordingly, on the very day after the momentous separation, Uncle Moses, Frank, and Bob started from Florence, without the slightest doubt that they would find David and Clive at Bologna. Before the boys had left, they had chosen from Murray's Handbook a certain hotel from among those that were specified therein; and it was to this that Uncle Moses at once went. Bologna looked as gloomy to these as it did to the others; and the drizzling rain, and the cloudy sky, and the general gloom still continued. As they drove to the hotel, Frank and Bob thought of sunny Florence, and groaned. At length they reached their destination, and hurrying in, they looked about eagerly, half expecting to find the objects of their search. They were disappointed, however, and then they proceeded to make inquiries about them.

The reply which they received was one that filled the questioners with amazement, and gave a dreadful shock to the anxious Uncle Moses.

"O, dey af gone," said the landlord, who was able to 'spik Ingelis;' "dey af gone, yesteda."

"Gone!" cried Frank. "Where?"

He half expected to hear that they had gone back to Florence in disgust.

"To Ferrara," said the landlord.

"Ferrara!" cried Frank; and he gave a low whistle.

"O, dey will come back," said the landlord; "dey say so; dey will come back."

"O, they'll come back — will they?" said Frank. "When? To-day?"

"O, yes, to-day, certamente," said the landlord; "dey say so."

This, at least, was some consolation.

"O, it's all right," said Frank, in a careless and confident tone, trying to cheer the wretched Uncle Moses. "You see, Uncle Mo, they couldn't stand Bologna, and no wonder. It's a horrible hole; so they've gone on to Ferrara; quite right, too; but Ferrara's only a few miles off, and I dare say they'll be back this evening. Now, don't you fret, or worry, or bother about it in the least. They'll be back this evening all right. So cheer up, and don't bother."

Uncle Moses tried to cheer up, but with little success. Frank's words, however, gave him some hope, and with this he endeavored to sustain himself. But the task was hard, and the time between this and evening seemed long indeed. Upon further inquiry they learned that the evening train from Ferrara would arrive at seven o'clock, at which time all would be decided.

"We must wait till then," said Uncle Moses, sadly, " though I'd much rayther go right straight off to Ferrary : but bein' as thar's a chance of their comin' back, why, I suppose we'd best wait."

" But don't look so heart-broken, Uncle Moses," said Frank. " Do, for pity's sake. try to cheer up."

" O, don't mind me," said Uncle Moses ; " don't you mind me. You jest go off an' see the town, an' I'll stay in my room an' lay down, an' p'aps I'll get a little sleep."

" Yes, do," said Frank, eagerly. " Try to sleep. I don't believe you slept a wink all last night."

They were now shown to their rooms, and the boys, leaving Uncle Moses here, went out to see the city, and did not return till evening. Their opinion was the same as that which had been formed by Clive and David.

" It's a dull place," said Frank, " and I don't wonder they went to Ferrara, only I hope, for poor Uncle Mo's sake, that they'll be back to-night."

The train came in at the appointed time, and Frank and Bob were at the station to receive the returning wanderers. To their disappointment, however, they saw nothing of them, and when they returned, Uncle Moses read their feelings on their faces. He said not a word, but stood trembling and frightened.

"O, come now," said Frank, cheerfully, "don't be so agitated, Uncle Mo. The boys are all right. It's impossible that any harm can have come to them. They thought that they had two or three days to themselves, you see, and Bologna's so dull that they'll not come back here till the last moment. They'll be back some time to-morrow."

"Some time to-morrow!" said Uncle Moses. "Wal, I can't set down here and wait. I must go on, too, and meet them at Ferrary. And I'll leave a letter for them here, same as I did at Florence."

Uncle Moses was very much agitated, and did not say a great deal, but it was evident that he was busy with anxious thoughts. He wrote another letter here, which he deposited with the landlord, to be given to the boys in the event of their return, and then seemed to feel a little calmer.

Early on the following morning they left for Ferrara. On arriving at this place, they went first to the chief hotel, supposing that the boys would be more likely to have lodged here than anywhere else. Here they found their suppositions correct, for the familiar names were there on the book of visitors. But they were destined, nevertheless, to fresh disappointment. They were informed that the boys had remained but a few hours, and had gone on to Padua. They had left no word as to their return, or as to any further movements.

This information was a fresh blow to Uncle

Moses, and even Frank and Bob thought the situation serious. It was not at all like Clive and David. They were generally quiet, and not over-fond of adventures. Why they should now be transformed into lawless vagabonds was a mystery.

Frank saw, however, that Uncle Moses required all his care, for it seemed as though the aged man would sink under this new disappointment.

"I see how it is," said he, cheerfully. "They've gone all about Ferrara, and have concluded to visit Padua also before returning to Bologna. They could not have spent more than two hours here. I dare say they are now in Padua. But of course they'll be back in Bologna in time to meet us."

"But what can I do?" wailed Uncle Moses. "How can I ever see them again?"

"Well," said Frank, "it seems to me that our best plan will be to go back to Bologna, and wait there for them to return."

Uncle Moses groaned.

"I feel," said he, "jest as if them two had got a start, and were agoin' off never to return. I feel as if my only chance is to folly them as fast as I can, and catch up to them if possible. And so I don't seem to care about goin' back. My only idee is, to go for'ard and catch them before they're lost."

"When will you go?"

"Why, as soon as possible. You find out when the next train is goin' to start for Padua."

"The next train? Why, that leaves at two o'clock. I saw the time-table in the office."

" Two o'clock: very well," said Uncle Moses; " then we'll go on to Padua by that train."

" But suppose the boys go back to Bologna, when we're going to Padua."

" Wal, we can try Padua first," said Uncle Moses, " an' then, if we find they've gone back, we can go back, too. They'll get my letter at Bolony. I told them to wait at Bolony at all hazards, an' not to stir a step till we come back. An' so they'll stay there. At the same time, if we find them at Padua, it'll be so much the better."

This decision was not at all disagreeable to Frank and Bob. They had several hours to wait in Ferrara, and these they spent in going about the town. They were not fond of ruins, or of churches, or of museums ; they were not poetical or romantic, like David and Clive ; nor did they care for old associations, or historic names. The result was, that Ferrara seemed duller to them than it had been to David and Clive, and they both voted it a slow place.

" It's quite evident why they went on to Padua," said Frank.

" Yes," said Bob ; " they did quite right ; but I say, Frank, isn't it odd to think of solemn old David and quiet Clive running such a rig as this ? If we had done it, why, it would have seemed natural."

" Well," said Frank, " I don't think I should have done it. At any rate, I should have telegraphed to Uncle Moses at Florence, or, at least, I should have written. It's very careless in them. Of course they're all right, and they'll turn up somewhere : but meanwhile poor old Uncle Mo's fretting himself into a fever. Bother take them, I say."

At two o'clock they left Ferrara, and in a short time arrived at Padua. Here, as before, they went to the chief hotel in the city, and once more regained the track of the wanderers. But here, as before, they found that the wanderers had gone, and that this time they had proceeded to Venice.

At this information poor old Uncle Moses seemed utterly crushed, and even Frank and Bob felt something like consternation. Thus far they had felt as though their uncle's anxiety was quite unnecessary, since at all events the boys would certainly come back to Bologna ; but this last act put the whole matter upon quite a different footing. At Bologna they had known where to go ; at Ferrara and Padua their course had been easy, namely, to go to the principal hotel ; but what could they do now ? Venice had many hotels, from among which it was difficult to choose any one that seemed likely to be the abode of the fugitives. In addition to this, it was incomprehensible how David and Clive could ever have thought of going off in this fashion. There was no letter for them. The landlord knew nothing about their intended movements. The boys had plunged into utter obscurity. Uncle Moses was heart-broken, and Frank did not know how to console him. They had shown an utter recklessness, and at the same time a heartlessness which filled Frank with amazement, and added to the difficulty of the case.

Still it was necessary to decide upon some course of action. Uncle Moses seemed quite distracted with anxiety and terror, so that Frank had now to make all the plans for the future.

" I think," said he, " that our only course is to go on to Venice."

" What can we do in Venice ? " said Uncle Moses, in a hollow voice.

" Do ? " said Frank. " Why, we can hunt up Dave and Clive."

" It's like hunting for a needle in a haystack," said Bob.

Uncle Moses groaned.

" O, there needn't be any difficulty. We can get the police to hunt them up."

" The police ! " said Uncle Moses, in a voice of horror. " The police ! "

" Certainly," said Frank. " Why not? I've heard that the police at Venice are a very efficient body of men."

" So have I," groaned Uncle Moses. " That's jest what I've heerd all my life. The police at Venice. Why, Venice is a vast police station. It's filled with spies, an' bravos, an' assassins. Why, I mind readin' about it when I was a boy at school. The first novel I ever read was Abellino, the Bravo of Venice. And I've heerd about the dungeons thar, an' the terrible courts, an' the torments they make use of. O, I know all about it. Why, the Inquisition at Venice is the most horrible thing on airth. The idee of it used to keep me awake at night. It's like Fox's Book of Martyrs, or the Valley of the Shadow of Death. To go thar is like goin' straight into the jaws of Death."

"O, nonsense!" said Frank. "That is all old stuff. It might have been so in the middle ages, but Venice now is a quiet, easy-going city, as safe as Boston — part of the kingdom of Italy. At any rate, we've got to go."

"Well," said Uncle Moses, heroically, "we've got to go, an' for my part, I'd go after them boys, to save them, if it was into the dungeons of the Inquisition themselves. Yes," he added, "if I had to lie on the rack, or be tried by the Council of Ten, or be broken on the wheel, or burnt at the stake."

And so, while Clive and David were enjoying themselves hugely with their new friends at Venice, poor old Uncle Moses was overwhelmed with anxiety and terror at Padua.

CHAPTER VII.

The Pleasant Party in Venice. — How to find a Missing Relative. — The Story of the beheaded Doge.

ET us now return to the pleasant party in Venice.

On the next morning Vernon called on the Bureau of Police to see what had been done about Miss Lee. He learned that nothing had been done thus far, but that a messenger was about to start for Verona in an hour. This news he brought back to Gracie, who was very anxious to know whether anything had been heard.

She looked disappointed.

"I hoped," she said, with a little sigh, "that they might have telegraphed. Poor auntie will be in despair. And did they try to find whether she was in Venice or not?"

"O, yes. She is not here. She is, no doubt, in Verona, and will wait there till she hears about you. I dare say she will get the police to hunt you up and take you prisoner."

"And do you think, Mr. Vernon," asked Gracie, "that there is any chance of my hearing anything of her to-day?"

Vernon shook his head.

"I'm afraid not," said he. "The messenger will go to-day. He will hardly be able to find her in time to come back by the evening train. Still, it is possible, no doubt. But the best way is to allow ample time, and not to be impatient. Now, I do not see how the messenger can get back before to-morrow. And, besides, your aunt may refuse to come with him."

"Refuse! How could she?"

"O, I was merely thinking that she might be terrified at the idea of going with a policeman, especially to Venice. Venice has a bad name in those matters."

"Auntie's awfully timid," said Gracie. "At any rate she'll write, and I'll fly back to her."

"If I could only persuade your aunt to stay in Verona a little longer," said Vernon, "I would make a pilgrimage there, and get her consent — "

Gracie looked at him inquiringly; then her eyes fell.

"Why?" she said, in a little whisper.

"Why? Because we cannot bear to have our little circle broken up so soon, before we have begun to see Venice, too; and if you were to leave us now, why, you see, all our plans would be spoiled, and if I could only know that your aunt was safe, and if you, too, felt at ease about her, I should rather like the police to terrify her."

"I'm sure that's very unkind," said Gracie.

"I know it is," said Vernon, in a tone of profound compunction; "but it arises from my own wicked heart."

Gracie smiled at this, with a pretty air of confusion.

"At any rate," said she, "I shall hear from auntie to-morrow."

"O, yes, or the day after; and Clive here and Davie will hear, too, no doubt. By the by, boys, what address did you give your uncle?"

"Poste Restante," said David.

"O, so you did not mention the Hotel Zeno."

"No," said David, "I did not feel certain about staying here, and thought 'Poste Restante' would be the safest and most convenient address."

"But suppose he comes on himself, how will he find you?"

"O, he won't come on," said Clive; "he'll write first, of course. Besides, Frank and Bob will be delighted to hear what we have done, and will tease Uncle Moses to spend another week in Florence. You know they're crazy about Florence."

"O, well," said Vernon, "that's all the better. I only wish Miss Lee could feel as comfortable about her aunt. However, we have this day before us, and I've been making a plan of action. How would you like to see the city? and what do you say to visiting the Doge's Palace?"

"I have no choice," said Gracie. "I don't know anything about Venice, and shall be happy to go wherever you take me."

In a short time they set forth in a gondola, and went to the Piazza of St. Mark. Here they landed.

The Doge's Palace is a large edifice which extends from the Grand Canal to the Cathedral of St. Mark, overlooking the Piazza and the landing-place, or Piazzetta. The front is adorned with rows of columns and arches, which give it a Byzantine appearance. The entrance looks out upon the Piazza of St. Mark, and is approached by a noble stairway, known as the "Giant's Stairs." At the head of these are certain orifices representing the mouths of lions. These are the terrible "lions' mouths" into which secret accusations were once dropped. The "lions' mouths" and the "giant's stairs" figure largely in the legends and the history of Venice.

Here Vernon led his companions, and pointed out to them these things just mentioned. After this they entered the Palace, traversed the grand hall, and came to the Council Chamber. Here they saw magnificent paintings, and conspicuous among them the largest oil painting in the world — the work of Tintoretto. Then they visited many other apartments, including the Senate Chamber, and the Rooms of Audience. All these were magnificently furnished and adorned with paintings.

In one of these rooms they sat down. An open window commanded a fine view of the Piazza, with the lofty tower of St. Mark.

"Do you see the Giant's Stairs below," asked Vernon.

" Yes," said Gracie.

" I intend to be your guide, philosopher, and friend," said Vernon, " and so I must tell you all about the places of importance that we meet. Did you ever hear of Marino Faliero?"

" O, yes," said Gracie. " I've read Byron's play."

" It's all the same," said Vernon. " I'll tell you the story. I've brought it all written out, and if you care to hear it i will read it. Shall I? or will it be too much of a bore?"

" O, read it, by all means."

Upon this Vernon drew forth some papers, and began to read

The Story of Marino Faliero.

The formation of the Council of Ten had the effect of diminishing the power of the other parts of the government. In particular the office of chief magistrate had been affected by it, and the Doge of Venice at length became little more than a mere name.

It was about forty years after the establishment of the Council of Ten that Marino Faliero was elected doge. He was one of the most distinguished citizens of Venice, sprung from one of the noblest families, and with a name rendered illustrious by glorious achievements in war. and skilful administration of civil affairs.

The ducal dignity, which had appeared so brilliant an object of ambition, was no sooner attained, than Marino Faliero found it nothing better than a splendid mockery. In most of the affairs of state he was allowed to do nothing whatever. He was subjected to the most galling control, not only in public matters, but even in those things which pertained to his private affairs. To add to all, spies were set around him, and he found that the position of first citizen of Venice was only that of a state prisoner.

Accustomed all his life to command; possessed of great self-reliance and resolution; animated, also, by honorable pride and ambition, Marino Faliero no sooner found out the truth of this position than he sought for some remedy. Circumstances hastened his search. Not only was he harassed by the espionage and restraint of the Council of Ten, but he also found that he was actually exposed to insult. On one occasion this insult was more bitter than usual, since it was aimed not at himself, but at his wife. The offence could not be overlooked. Unable to punish the offender himself, he denounced him to the Council. The result was, that the Council punished the accused by a sentence of imprisonment for two months, to be followed by banishment for one year. To the doge this punishment appeared so inadequate to the offence that he regarded it almost as an indorsement by the Council of the insult. His haughty spirit could not endure it any longer, and he now looked about for means to avenge himself.

The opportunity soon presented itself. On the day after the sentence a high noble came to him to seek reparation for a blow which he had received from another noble. " What can I do for you," said Faliero ; " think of the shameful insult that has been offered me, and the way in which they have punished that ribald who wrote it; and see how the Council respect my person." Upon this, the other said, eagerly, " My Lord Doge, if you wish to make yourself a real prince, and destroy all these your enemies, I have the courage, if you will help me, to make you chief of the whole state, and then you can punish all of them."

Faliero at once fell in with the proposal, and soon a conspiracy was organized. His nephew, Bertucci, and Calendaro, a distinguished naval commander, who had formerly served under Faliero, were sent for to take part in the plot. Six others were taken into the affair, and for many nights in succession the scheme was discussed in the Ducal Palace, until at length the whole was decided. It was arranged that sixteen or seventeen leaders should be posted in various parts of the city, each at the head of forty armed men, who, however, were not to know their destination. On the appointed day they were to raise riots among themselves in order that the doge might have a pretence for tolling the bell of St. Mark. At the sound of the bell the whole band was to gather at St. Mark's, and when the citizens should come to

know the cause of the alarm, the conspirators were
to fall upon them and cut them to pieces. After
this Faliero was to be proclaimed Lord of Venice.
The day appointed for the rising was the 15th of
April, 1355; and so profound was the secrecy
which was maintained that no one dreamed of the
existence of the conspiracy.

But on the evening before the appointed day,
one of the conspirators, being anxious to save a
dear friend from danger, went to see him and earnestly entreated him to remain at home on the mor-
row. The friend, astonished at the singular request,
began to make inquiries of his visitor, and though
the latter at first tried to maintain secrecy, yet at
length he told all. The friend was filled with horror: he at once arrested his informant, and then,
having secured him, he hurried forth to inform
the magistrates. These immediately procured the
arrest of all the members of the conspiracy, who
were captured at their own houses. Guards were
then placed at the arsenal, and distributed through
the city. For these the punishment was plain and
easy, but with the doge it would be more difficult
to deal.

The Council of Ten, therefore, demanded the
assistance of twenty nobles, who were to advise, but
not to vote. They then sent for the doge, who had
heard nothing whatever of the disclosure of the
conspiracy, and was arrested in the midst of his
palace, while friends, and guests, and visitors were
all around him.

The fact of his arrest was enough. That one thing told him all that had occurred. On being brought before the dread tribunal, he said not a word, neither denying the charge nor seeking to excuse himself. He was accordingly found guilty, and condemned to be beheaded, the place of execution to be the landing-place of the Giant's Stairs, where the doges take their oath when they first enter the palace.

When the execution was over, one of the Council of Ten went to the columns of the palace opposite the Piazza, and holding up the bloody sword, cried out, "Justice has fallen on the traitor!" and the gates being then opened, the people rushed in to see the doge who had been executed.

"O, thank you very much," said Gracie, as Vernon paused. "It brings back all Byron's play, though your story presents the doge in a different light. But then poets have to depart a little from the actual facts of the case."

"Certainly," said Vernon. "A poet is like an artist, and has often to sacrifice truth to artistic effect. But of course the moral is the same."

"O, yes, I dare say it is," said Gracie. "I take your word for it, especially since you put it in that way. I did not think of that before. There always seemed to me something wrong in a poet's departure from the truth; but now that you call him an artist, and speak about the artistic effect, it seems

very different indeed.   And, in fact, the poet must
do so, for it is his art that makes the difference between poetry and prose."

"Are you an artist?" asked Vernon.

"O, no," said Gracie; "I should not venture to
call myself an artist.   I can draw a little, and paint
a little, and — "

"I wish I could see some of your work," said
Vernon, eagerly.   "I should love to see some of
your work.   I dare say I could give you some
hints — "

"O, I would give anything to have you give me
some hints," responded Gracie, with equal eagerness.   "There are a thousand things that I want to
know about, and — but what's the use?" she added,
in a mournful voice, "when there's poor, dear
auntie, and — but if she were only here, and
safe!"

"I declare," said Vernon, "I've a great mind to
start off this afternoon by the train and hunt her
up myself.   But then —"   He stopped abruptly.

"O, I should think the police would be better
able to find her than you could be," said Gracie.

"I would go at once," said Vernon, in a low
voice, "but then there is a reason — "

"What?" asked Gracie, innocently.

"Why, I don't want to break up our little circle,
and," he added, in a lower voice, "I don't want to
go away from *you*."

CHAPTER VIII.

*The Dungeons of the Inquisition. — The Bridge of Sighs. —
The Story of a Life-long Vengeance.*

URING this conversation David and Clive
had wandered off up and down the long
corridor. After a time Vernon and Gracie
came towards them, and said that they were going
to visit the dungeons of the Inquisition.

" This Inquisition," said Vernon, " isn't the Holy
Office of the Inquisition, of which you have heard
so much; it had no connection with the Roman
Catholic church, or with religion. It was the Inquisition of the Venetian state, and by Inquisition
is meant simply the criminal court. The name has
misled many; but though the Venetian Inquisition
was a civil court, yet the horrors perpetrated by it
were fully equal to any that were ever done by its
terrible sister, the Holy Office — the Inquisition of
Spain."

" Or of Rome," said Clive.

" O, no," said Vernon; " the Inquisition at Rome
was but a feeble concern compared with this one.
But come, let us see what there is left of it. One
look, I think, will be enough to put an end to all
romantic regrets for the fate of Venice."

They now went on, and came to a large apartment, quite as large as the Council Chamber, and furnished quite as magnificently. This was the Hall of the Inquisition. Leaving this, they descended a narrow flight of stone steps, and came to a passage-way which was lighted by a small window.

Here Vernon stopped.

"Can you guess where we are?" he asked.

"No."

"This is the Bridge of Sighs," he said.

"The Bridge of Sighs!" repeated the others, in wonder.

"Yes; look out of that window, and you can see the canal beneath."

A stool was there, by standing on which they could see that it was so.

After this they went on, and came into the terrible prison-house. Upon the story which was on a level with the bridge, they saw narrow cells, lighted only by a small hole in each door. These were dismal enough, but were the best of all. Taking lights, they went down a narrow stone stairway, and found themselves on a lower story, where the dungeons were smaller, and darker, and more repellent. But these were not the worst, for beneath these they found others in the lowest story of all. These lay beneath the level of the sea. and there was something in them so appalling that they retreated after a very short examination. There was a sense of horror over the visitors, and none of them felt able to breathe freely until they had come back to their old station at the balcony.

"If you like," said Vernon, "I will read you another story, which is associated with these horrible prisons."

"O, do," said Gracie.

Vernon again read.

The Story of the Two Foscari.

The reign of the Doge Francesco Foscari extended over thirty-five years, which had been marked by constant wars, during which he had shown unusual ability in the management of affairs. His courage, firmness, and wisdom had made him illustrious; and under his rule Venice had increased in power, in territory, and in glory. Yet all these things could not save him from the dread power of the Ten; and in his history may be found the most awful example of that dark and baleful tyranny under which Venice had sunk—a tyranny which pressed heavily on all classes; which sacrificed innocent men to the spite of anonymous informers, and inflicted the pangs of unspeakable torment on the noblest in the state, at the instigation of personal malignity.

Twice in the course of his reign, Foscari had handed in his resignation. It had been refused, and on the second resignation an oath was exacted from him that he would retain his unwelcome dignity for life.

Three out of four sons were dead; and the one who survived, Giacopo, was a youth of noble qualities, before whom was the prospect of a splendid career. He had been married to a lady of the illustrious house of Contarini, and the aged doge looked to this last surviving son for the support of his declining years.

Suddenly the blow fell; which, awful as it was, proved to be but the first in a series of calamities, the very mention of which is terrible to every generous heart. Giacopo was denounced to the Council of Ten for having received presents from a foreign potentate. The offence, if true, was but a trifling one, and was probably not true at all; but before the Council of Ten accusation was enough. It was their fashion not to confront the accused with the accuser, but to examine him by torture; and in this instance the unhappy youth was put on the rack, and submitted to the question. The agonized father had to be present at this scene. This was part of the hellish device of the miscreant who had accused Giacopo. He cared not whether the accused was condemned or acquitted. He counted at least on having him subjected to the torture, and on inflicting worse torture on the wretched father. And so, on the rack, the young man confessed to the crime; and the father had to announce to him the sentence by which he was banished for life. Afterwards, at the special prayer of the doge, his wife was allowed to accompany him.

Several years passed, and Giacopo remained in banishment; when an event occurred which brought down a fresh calamity upon the wretched son and father. One of the Council of Ten was assassinated. On that day the servant of Giacopo had been seen in Venice. The Council, conscious of the horrible wrong which they had done, and suspecting vengeance from Foscari, at once re-called Giacopo from banishment to answer this new charge of treason and assassination.

Once more the hapless son was laid upon the rack, and once more the wretched father had to preside, and see the agony of one dearer than life, — his only son, — innocent of the charge, tortured by fiends from whom he could not save him. For the doge was but a name, and the Council of Ten held all power in their hands. Nevertheless, in spite of the torment, Giacopo continued firm in the protestation of his innocence; and the extremest torture was unavailing to extort from him a single word.

Yet, although proof was wanting, the Council of Ten declared him guilty, and attributed his silence to the effect of witchcraft and magic. Once more, therefore, they condemned him, and this time they banished him to a more remote place in Candia. For a while he was insane through his sufferings in body and mind; and though his innocence was proved by the discovery of the real assassin, still no change was made in his sentence; and on the recovery of his reason he was sent to Candia. To add to it all, this time his wife was not allowed to accompany him.

"Alone in this far-distant land, the miserable Giacopo fell a victim to pining homesickness. Death seemed preferable to this, when life was intolerable; and at last, in his despair, he wrote a letter to the Duke of Milan, entreating his intercession with the Venetian government, so that he might return home, even as a prisoner.

This letter was discovered by the Venetian spies, and the result was, that he was brought home; but it was on the charge of treasonable correspondence with a foreign state. This charge meant a fresh trial and renewed torture.

Once more, and for a third time, the miserable Giacopo was subjected to the torture; and the miserable father, in the hideous mockery of the ducal dignity, was compelled to preside. For no less than thirty times was the poor victim stretched upon the rack; but no torment could wring from him a confession of guilt. At last, all torn, bleeding, dislocated, and senseless, he was carried away. The doge was allowed to visit him in his cell. The wretched father tried to console his son, but fell senseless in his agony.

All this, however, had not the slightest effect on the Council of Ten. Giacopo was once more punished by banishment, and once more he left his beloved home for far-distant Candia, where he died shortly after his arrival.

The miserable father, to whom death would have been welcome, continued to live on. He was compelled to retain his dignity of doge, but he lived secluded, and never attended any more councils. His heart was broken, and there was nothing left for him now but to wait patiently for that death which could not be long delayed.

At length a proposal was made for the deposition of the doge. Some debate followed, and at length it was agreed to. So they declared the office of doge vacant, ordered him to quit the palace within three days, and added to this the vote of a trifling pension.

Foscari received the announcement with calmness. He laid aside the ducal robes, and prepared to go. It was suggested that he should leave by the private stairway, but this he refused. " No," said he, " I will descend by the same steps by which I mounted thirty-five years ago."

With these words he went forth, and, supported by his brother, he slowly descended the Giant's Stairs.

Five days afterwards the bell of St. Mark tolled to announce the election of a new doge. Its sounds penetrated to the ears of Foscari. It brought before him all his wrongs and sufferings. He started up in unutterable anguish at the recollection that crowded upon him ; some inarticulate words escaped him ; but before the peal of the bell had ceased, he fell down dead.

It is evident that such wrongs as these of the two Foscari must have arisen from something more than the wanton exercise of tyranny on the part of the Council of Ten. This dread tribunal has crimes enough and horrors enough to answer for; but in this case it has only a part of the guilt that arises from these cruelties. There was one who stood behind them, the secret mover, who, in all his acts, was but following the impulse of a life-long trust for vengeance. That one was Loredano.

He belonged to a family which had an hereditary feud with that of the Foscari. His uncle, who had gained high distinction as admiral, was so hostile to Foscari, that the latter once declared that he should never be doge so long as Pietro Loredano lived. Shortly after this the admiral died suddenly, it was rumored by poison. His brother also died shortly after, in the same sudden way, and rumor also attributed this to poison. Loredano thus lost his father and his uncle. He believed that Foscari had effected their destruction in this way. Upon his father's tomb he caused the inscription to be placed that he had died by poison; and from that time he devoted his whole life to the one purpose of vengeance.

At length he found himself in authority as one of the Council of Ten — that supreme tribunal, before whom the doge himself was but a weak tool. Here he had occasion to use the tremendous power which had been placed in his hands, and there was not a pang that the Foscari suffered which was not marked by him as so much satisfaction given to his desire for revenge.

Like most of the Venetian nobles, Loredano was engaged in commerce. When he heard of the death of Foscari, he took down one of his ledgers, and turned to a page where there was an entry among his list of debtors.

" Francesco Foscari, for the death of my father and uncle."

He took his pen, and calmly wrote on the other side, —

" By his death."

As Vernon ended, he turned over a leaf of his manuscript, and showed a page which was ruled so as to represent the page of a merchant's ledger, with entries of debit and credit, such as Loredano might have had before him when he balanced his account with Foscari.

Dr.	Francesco Foscari.	Cr.
For the death of my uncle. For the death of my father.		By 3 tortures of son Giacopo and self. By his deposition. By his death. (Debt paid in full.)

CHAPTER IX.

*A Race three hundred Feet up into the Air. ··· The Story
of the Origin of Venice. — The Story of the jealous
Artist.*

"SHOULD you like to go to the top of the
tower of St. Mark?" asked Vernon of
Gracie.

"O, yes," was the reply, "very, very much. I
should like it above all things."

"But it's a very great thing to do," said Vernon.
"It's very much higher than Bunker Hill Monu-
ment."

"O, but I'm a capital climber," said Gracie. "I
assure you, Mr. Vernon, I should like it above all
things."

"O, then, if that's your state of mind, we must
go at once," said Vernon.

Leaving the doge's palace they crossed over to
the Tower of St. Mark, which was only a short
distance away, and began the long ascent. Dave
and Clive dashed away, and ran a race to the top,
while Vernon and Gracie walked more slowly.
Vernon was determined that Gracie should not fatigue herself, and insisted that she should take his

arm. This Gracie positively refused to do; but at length, as Vernon made such a point of it, she consented. The ascent wound round and round in a spiral way: it was very gradual and very easy, yet, such was Vernon's anxious solicitude about Gracie that he made her stop more than twenty times on the way up, so as to avoid all fatigue. In this way they went up, and reached the top long after Clive and David: but Gracie was not in the least tired, and her flushed cheeks and sparkling eyes showed that the ascent had been beneficial rather than exhaustive.

On looking out from their lofty position, they beheld, on every side, a most magnificent view. Beneath lay Venice, the peerless city of the sea, with the water all around. Yet from this height they were not able to see many of the canals, for the lofty houses concealed all of them except the Grand Canal, and one or two others that were close by them. Towards the east lay the broad Adriatic, with a blue line along the horizon, showing the coast of Dalmatia; on the west they saw the plains of Italy; on the north, the mountains; while on the south the sea faded away till in the distance it blended with the horizon.

Perhaps the most wonderful thing of all was the deep silence that prevailed. All was still. There was no rumble from carriage-wheels, none of that uproar which marks every other city. It seemed like a city of the dead.

"Haven't you some more stories in that manuscript of yours?" asked Gracie, after she had seen all that was to be seen.

"O, yes," said Vernon, "lots of them ; but I don't know which to choose. I wish to choose something appropriate. Let me see. It seems to me that the best thing to read just now is about the origin of Venice."

So Vernon went on to read

THE ORIGIN OF VENICE.

The name of Venice is derived from that of the Veneti, a people who lived upon the adjoining main land, under the Roman empire. During the decline of that power, they suffered much from various invaders, until at length the approach of Attila, "the Scourge of God," sent many of them to seek for refuge in some place which would be less liable to the ravages of hostile bands. Such a place they found in a cluster of little islands which lay a few miles out at sea, at the head of the Adriatic. Defended by the sea from the armies that ravaged Italy, they were also equally well defended from piratical ships or hostile fleets, by sandbanks and shoals that could only be traversed through channels of the most intricate character. This, then, was the place which the fugitive Veneti chose for their refuge ; and here they settled upon one of the largest islands, which bore the name of Rialto. It was on the 25th of March, 452, when this first settlement was made. Numerous bands of people followed, settling upon adjoining islands, and the little community thus began that career which was destined to be so splendid. Though a part of the Roman empire, the Veneti governed themselves, and were but rarely troubled by the agents of the emperor. They had what was virtually a free republic; and thus, with the great blessings of freedom and safety, together with a good government, and law, and order, they were in a condition which, in comparison with that of other cities, may justly be called most enviable.

Time passed on, and at length large numbers of fugitives again came out to settle upon neighboring islands. These were driven away by the advance of Alboin at the head of his Lombards. The new settlements, after a time, became connected with the old one : and at length, in the year 697, the necessity was felt of a regular organized government which should blend them all into one state. Twelve of the principal men were empowered to choose a ruler, and this one thus elected was called the Doge or Duke of Venice.

Venice now went on increasing in population, extending its commerce, and developing its naval power. During the eighth and ninth centuries, the ravages of the Saracens filled all Christendom with terror; but Venice remained secure. More than this, the common danger seemed to bring forth more prominently the strength of this young city of the seas, to draw forth her resources, and strengthen her maritime power. In one great struggle of the Italians against the Eastern Roman Empire, the Venetian fleet took a prominent part, and gained a decisive victory; while her next great victory was gained over the ruler of the new-risen Western Roman Empire, the mighty Charlemagne. In this struggle the fleet of the emperor, which was commanded by his son Pepin, was defeated.

In the year 809 the government was made stronger. By this time no less than sixty islands were united in the city of Venice. Her commerce extended far and wide; her maritime power was sufficient to insure her the command of the Adriatic Sea: and already the wealth and power of the young republic were visible in splendid edifices.

Her power now continued to increase. Towards the end of the tenth century the cities of Dalmatia put themselves under her protection. At the end of the eleventh century the crusades began, and these mighty movements acted directly and immediately upon Venice, increasing her population, extending her commerce, enlarging her naval power, and developing to an immense extent all her resources. It was during this period that she attained to her highest glory. She became the Queen of the Adriatic, the conqueror of the capital of the East, the chief of all the cities on earth, when —

> " her daughters had their dowers
> From spoils of nations, and the exhaustless East
> Poured in her lap all gems in sparkling showers.
> In purple was she robed, and of her feast
> Monarchs partook, and deemed their dignity increased.
>
> In youth she was all glory — a new Tyre;
> Her very by-word sprung from victory,
> The ' Planter of the Lion,' which through fire
> And blood she bore o'er subject earth and sea;
> Though making many slaves, herself still free,
> And Europe's bulwark 'gainst the Ottomite;
> Witness Troy's rival, Candia! Vouch it, ye
> Immortal waves, that saw Lepanto's fight!
> For ye are names no time nor tyranny can blight."

"Thank you," said Gracie; "that's very nice. It isn't tragic. It isn't exciting. It's simply nice. It's so full of information, and all that, you know. But as to your quotation from Byron, I think that it is not so effective just now as it ought to be."

" Why not?"

" O, well, you know, after one has just emerged from the dungeons of the Inquisition, and has all the horror about one, why, one has no patience with Venice. To indulge in lamentations over her fall seems rather out of place. For how can one feel like lamenting the fall of a state which was built upon a system of wrong, and baseness, and hideous cruelty? The names of the two Foscari are enough to put one out of conceit with Venice forever."

"To tell the truth," said Vernon, " that is exactly my own feeling, and I have no sympathy whatever with Childe Harold's lamentations over Venice."

"I suppose," said Gracie, "we must regard all that as the poet's art."

"You have the idea exactly," said Vernon. "You are so quick at catching hints, and so apt, that I long to have you for my pupil, if it were only for a short time; for I know that you would make the most brilliant progress."

"But, then, there's poor dear auntie!" said Gracie, with a little sigh. "O, if she were only here! or somewhere so that I could hear from her!"

After seeing all that was to be seen, they descended. Clive and David, as before, ran a race down. Clive had beaten in the race up. He had passed David not long after starting, and thinking that David was close behind, had run all the way. The exertion was tremendous, and he had reached the top in such a state of exhaustion that it was long before he could recover his breath; and even then he felt in that condition which is usually termed shaky. As for David, he soon gave up the race, and, after Clive had passed, he slackened his pace to a moderate walk. He was rewarded for this, for on the race down Clive soon gave out; but David, being quite fresh, kept ahead, and reached the bottom long before his rival.

As for Vernon and Gracie, they did not think of racing, or hurrying in any way. Vernon insisted again on her taking his arm, so that she might be saved from the fatigue of the descent; and Gracie again, after a first refusal, accepted the offer.

Then they came down very leisurely, — so leisurely, in fact, that Clive and David grew tired with waiting for them.

On reaching the bottom, Vernon proposed a visit to some picture galleries, as this would be an easy and pleasant way of passing the remainder of the day. This, of course, was an agreeable proposal, and they were soon seated in the gondola on their way to the Academy of Fine Arts. It was a noble edifice, superbly furnished, and filled with great paintings, the crown and glory of which was the famous "Assumption" of Titian. Vernon pointed out the peculiar qualities of this great master, and had many stories to tell relative to his life and character.

Leaving this, they visited the Pisano and Barberigo Palaces, and at length they came to the Palazzo Manfrini. This was a marble edifice of great beauty, containing a collection of pictures as extensive and as excellent as that of the Academy of Fine Arts. The pictures represented many artists, and many schools of painting. Vernon showed them works of Titian, of Tintoretto, of Rubens, of Rembrandt, and many others, pointing out the distinguishing features of each. From a few words and simple explanations thus made by a skilful artist in the presence of the pictures themselves, Gracie learned more than she could have gained from prolonged study of mere books.

At length they sat down by a window which

looked out upon the Grand Canal, and here once more Vernon produced his manuscript.

"If you care about it," he said, "I will read you a story. It's not about statesmen, or soldiers; it's about artists."

The others received his proposal with much pleasure, and thereupon Vernon read

The Story of Daru and Priuli.

Daru and Priuli had been rivals in youth, but Priuli had distanced the other, and his superior genius was manifest. For this Daru could never forgive him; and as Priuli went on in the full tide of honor and fortune, Daru never ceased to feel the bitterest jealousy, accompanied by a fierce thirst for vengeance on the man whose only offence had been his superior abilities. Outwardly, however, Daru professed a warm and admiring friendship; and Priuli, who was too successful to feel jealous himself, was slow to suspect jealousy in others. So he gave Daru credit for all the friendship that he professed, which friendship the other tried to make as intimate as possible. Flattery of Priuli and depreciation of himself were the means which he employed, and in this way he so won upon the other's good will, that his confidence followed as a matter of course. And now, having gained this much, Daru watched every act of Priuli, in the hope that something would take place which might put him in his power. Still the task was a tedious one.

For a simple artist like Priuli, an offence against the laws was hardly possible. He had no vices. He lived frugally. He made no debts, nor did he ever gamble. All the ordinary ways by which one man may lead another to ruin were thus closed to Daru, who found himself compelled to trust to the chapter of accidents. Even the quietest and most innocent men, thought Daru, will often do things that may be distorted so as to seem like offences of great magnitude; all that I need is patience; something must occur at last.

At last something did occur. A French noble residing at Venice had engaged Priuli to paint him a picture, which Priuli had finished and had taken to his lodgings. It happened that war suddenly broke out between France and Venice consequent upon the famous League of Cambray, and the French noble found himself compelled to return home. At the same time all his financial resources were cut off, owing to the war; and for the same reason he found it impossible to obtain money from the brokers. In this emergency Priuli urged him to take the picture and send him the money at some future time. The French noble did so, and Priuli knew that the debt would be paid, as the rank and wealth of the debtor placed him beyond the reach of suspicion. His confidence was well founded. Long before the time had ended which he had counted on as the probable duration of the debt, the money was sent to him. It came by a Venetian Jew, who had just returned from Milan, where he had been commissioned by the French noble to give the money to Priuli.

All this was well known to Daru. It seemed to him to be the very time for which he had been so long waiting. Accordingly he hastened to make a charge against Priuli, and dropped into the dread "Lion's Mouth" secret information that Priuli had received money from a foreign prince with whom Venice was at war.

Such a charge was a terrible one at all times. The law was strict, and was watched with jealous vigilance. On charges of this sort some of the highest and haughtiest nobles in Venice had been arrested and tried. Fame, rank, virtue, popularity, all had failed to save them. All this Daru well knew, and he thought that in a time like this such a charge against a private man like Priuli would be certain ruin.

This was the fearful system at Venice, that any man might gratify his spite by an anonymous denunciation of an enemy on any charge whatever. If the charge proved utterly unfounded, the prisoner was set free, yet reluctantly; for the Venetian government never let any one go free if they could possibly help it; while, if there were any ground whatever for the charge, the utmost efforts were put forth to extort a confession from the accused, and those efforts were generally the effective workings of the rack, or other instruments of torture.

So, when Daru learned that Priuli had been arrested, he felt sure that the charge would be sifted to the bottom; that the payment of money would be found out, and that in order to extort further confession, Priuli would undoubtedly be placed upon the rack.

And after that, thought Daru, he'll have to lie in some dungeon till he rots; or, if he does get out, his joints will be too sore to allow him to paint again. O, ho, my *Priulino! caro amico!* how do you like my Lady Rack?

Meanwhile Priuli had been arrested, and brought before his judges. His explanation was frank and simple. He had received no money from a foreign power, but had merely received payment of a debt from a private person. He told the whole story so that there could not be any doubt as to its truth in the minds of the judges.

Now, had Priuli been a powerful noble, with powerful enemies, there is no doubt that the charge could have been pressed most vehemently, and the rack would certainly have been applied. But Priuli was not a noble. He was a simple artist. He had no powerful enemies, and no one in authority felt it to be his interest to put him to the torture. Moreover, the Venetians were always tender to artists; and so, as there was no motive to condemn him, he was not condemned. At the same time it was not in accordance with their policy to set any prisoner free too quickly. The Venetian government lived, and moved, and had its being in a system of fiendish cruelty and never-ending terrorism, which was always carried out to the fullest possible extent. Priuli, therefore, after his examination, was remanded to his prison.

But the Venetian government, with its countless spies, kept note of all the doings of the people. Seldom was it that any one was denounced without their finding out who the informant was. Their policy was to question the prisoner as to all his friends and associates, his business, his acts, and even his thoughts. From all these they could judge with cool and subtle penetration as to the motives of the information, and the name of the informer. So it was in this case; and it did not require much acuteness to perceive that Daru was the enemy.

The Venetians, moreover, were a commercial people, and always sought to get the greatest possible benefit from the smallest possible outlay. It seemed shocking to all principles of business to let a man like Priuli live in idleness in a dungeon, when he might be so much better employed. And so, being in want of a picture for the Ducal Palace, they gave him a commission to paint one of a certain size upon some event in Venetian history. He was removed to a comfortable room, where he could work at his ease, and everything was furnished him which he desired. In this way they accomplished many things. They retained the prisoner in his prison, yet they made that prisoner as comfortable as a free man. They also utilized his genius and his industry in their own behalf, and by giving him agreeable employment prevented him from sinking into despondency.

Meanwhile Daru was exulting in the completeness of his vengeance. He thought of Priuli, racked, tormented, prostrated in body and mind, no longer able to outshine him. Even if he should now be freed, he thought, he can no longer have the mind to conceive or the hand to execute. This would make him the first artist in Venice, and to him would come all those lucrative orders which had formerly fallen to the lot of Priuli. With these thoughts he solicited from the government a commission for the execution of that very work, which, unknown to him, had already been intrusted to Priuli. He had heard that the work had been decided on, and thought that he had the best claim to it.

His request was granted. At the same time certain conditions were imposed. Another artist, he was told, had already been engaged; but the government was willing to let him take it if he would consent to let its acceptance be subject to the approval of a committee which should judge between his work and that of the other artist.

To this Daru gladly consented. Who the other artist might be did not concern him in the least. He supposed him to be some rising artist under the patronage of some eminent noble, who had obtained the work for him.   But now that Priuli was gone, there was not one among the artists of Venice who could compete with himself.

He set to work, labored diligently, and at length his picture was completed.   It represented a scene from Venetian history — Carlo Zeno wounded at Chiozza.

A deputation came to see it, and were lavish in their expressions of praise.   At the same time they informed him that the other artist had completed his, and had sent it to the Ducal Palace.   They added that it had been much admired, and courteously invited him to go with them and see it. Such an invitation was not to be declined, and so Daru went with them.   As he went he felt strange and dismal forebodings.   He wondered how it was that the other picture should already be at the palace.   Had they chosen it before seeing his? Or was there something beneath all this?   The suspicious nature of Daru was aroused, but there was nothing to be done.

On reaching the Ducal Palace he was called into a large upper room in the left wing.   Here he saw a brilliant company assembled.   Among them were the doge himself and the chief counsellors. But in that company he saw one form which made him blind to all the rest.   Forgetting the reverence due to this august company, he stood rigid, and staring, with his eyes fixed upon the face of that

man whom for months he had thought of as languishing in a drear dungeon.

"We have given you a commission, signor," said
the doge, "but we had previously given it to
another, with whom you were to compete. We
honor our Priuli so much that we have invited him
to our own Ducal Palace to do his work undis-
turbed. His work is finished. It is here. Come
and see whether you think that yours is equal to
this."

Trembling and distracted with conflicting emo-
tions, the wretched Daru could neither speak nor
move. His base plot had been discovered. The
accused had been absolved and raised to honor;
he, the informer, had been detected and mocked.
Mocked! And was that all? Would that it were.
But he was here before the dread Council, and the
awful prison-house was near.

"This," continued the doge, "is an admirable
picture, a masterpiece, which shall adorn our walls.
As to your work, why, you shall be rewarded — for
all that you have done."

There was a terrible meaning in these words.
As the doge ended, he made a sign to the attend-
ants, and they led Daru away.

Priuli was restored to liberty in a few days,
but Daru, after having been kept in prison for about
a year, left Venice, and never came back.

CHAPTER X.

Another Call on the Police, with the Result thereof. --- The Story of the ambitious Money-Lender and his malignant Plot.

FTER quitting the Palazzo Manfrini, they went home. Leaving his friends here, Vernon proceeded to the Bureau of Police in order to find out whether they had received any information from Verona. The answer was neither satisfactory nor encouraging. They had heard nothing from their messenger, and they could not give any idea of the time when they would hear. It struck Vernon that there was an unpleasant air of indifference about these gentlemen of the police ; and there was a vague impression made upon his mind that perhaps they expected to be paid for these labors, which were outside of their usual routine. Had Vernon been in the possession of his usual presence of mind, he would have understood the situation at once, and have taken the hint which these noble gentlemen of the police were not slow to give. He would have feed them liberally all round, and then — why, the business would have been promptly performed, and this story would have taken a different turn altogether. But Vernon was not at all his usual self. He was absent-minded; his thoughts went wool-gathering; moreover, he did not feel any very great anxiety to bring the business to an end. The fact was, he was infatuated about Gracie, and his present situation was so delightful that he dreaded any change. The advent of Gracie's aunt upon the scene might put an end to his pleasant wanderings with her. The aunt might be grim, and precise, and rigid, and over-particular, and therefore he dreaded her arrival. He certainly did all that was befitting; but he did not show that fertility of resource, that energy and zeal, which he would have exhibited under different circumstances. And so he did not fee the police, and the police, as will afterwards appear, were languid in their efforts; and Gracie's aunt remained hidden under a dense cloud, and Vernon had to console Gracie as best he could.

He explained to Gracie that everything was going on well, but that as yet no tidings had been received. He showed, however, that there had not yet been sufficient time to hear anything, and encouraged her by the assurance that in a day or two all would be well. He urged her to think of Italy as she would think of Massachusetts, and declared that no danger could possibly befall any one.

"In a day or two," said he, "you will see her.

It'll take a day for the messenger to get to Verona and start the Verona police on the search; well, that's what has been done to-day: another day will be needed to find her: no more than that, I should think, will be necessary: well, that's to-morrow: the third day will be taken up with her journey here, or else with the sending of a message to you. And so, you know, I really don't see any cause for anxiety."

In spite of these confident assurances, however, Gracie did feel anxious — very anxious.

" It isn't because I'm afraid of any danger happening to her, Mr. Vernon," she said; " but I fear very much that her anxiety about me will make her ill. She is very much inclined to worry about things, and to lose me in this way is something terrible. O, 1 think 1 ought to have gone back to Verona."

" To Verona ! " said Vernon, aghast. " O, no — no, no. You did exactly right. For after all, your aunt may come here, and if so, she will communicate with the police at once, and will find you without any trouble. O, no ; it would have been madness for you to go back to Verona."

In this way Vernon succeeded in quelling the fears of Gracie, and after this he tried to divert her thoughts from so painful a subject by turning them to other things. He had other pictures to show her, he said, about which he wished to have her opinion. There were two in particular, and each of these was connected with a story, which story he had written out in his manuscript. The mention of this excited Gracie's curiosity, and Vernon produced the pictures, while Gracie, and David, and Clive all looked at them with the deepest interest.

The first one was called "The Lion's Mouth." It represented a man dropping a paper into that awful receptacle. The paper was supposed to contain a denunciation of some one. The face of the informer was turned towards the spectator, as his hand dropped the paper, and there was upon it a marvellous portrayal of hate, fear, vigilance, revenge, together with cunning, and vulgar exultation. It was a mean and contemptible face, and the skill of the artist was shown in his subtile delineation of these mingled passions.

They all looked at this picture with the deepest interest and admiration.

"You do not know what it is about," said Vernon.

"O, yes," said Gracie; "the picture is eloquent. It tells all; but of course it does not tell the names and the minor incidents, and so, if you are not tired, and are willing to read us one of your stories, I'm sure we should all feel very much obliged."

"Of course," said Vernon, "if you are willing to listen, I shall be very happy to read the story."

Saying this, he read from his manuscript the story of

MEMMO AND VALIERO.

The Venetian republic was a nation of shop-keepers. In this commercial state nearly all the nobles were engaged in trade; and from them arose the name Merchant Princes. Dealers in money arose, and throve among them at an early period. In the twelfth century a bank was established, — the first in the world, — which flourished for centuries before any other land had a similar institution. Private money-lenders, usurers, and brokers were as common at Venice in the middle ages as they are now, in the nineteenth century, in London. Money was subject to the same fluctuations. Hard times came and went. The rate of interest varied, and all sorts of contrivances were resorted to for the sake of obtaining the needful.

Conspicuous among these Venetian bankers was Memmo, a self-made man, who had risen from nothing, and by a long course of prosperous speculation and money-lending had made himself wealthy. Many nobles were among his debtors, and among those who were deepest on his books was Valiero, a member of one of the proudest families in the state. Like most other nobles, he was engaged in business; but various misfortunes had overtaken him, and he was compelled to raise money by all the wretched devices known to men in difficulties. From Memmo he had obtained what he wanted, and in return had mortgaged his houses and estates,

and had given his obligations for immense sums.
At last it seemed to Memmo that Valiero was completely in his power, and that the time had come
for broaching a plan which had been in his mind
for years.

Memmo was ambitious. He had gained wealth,
but that was not enough. He wished to obtain
social distinction. For this he was willing to make
pecuniary sacrifices to almost any extent. The
misfortunes of Valiero and his immense debts
seemed to open a way for the accomplishment of
his wishes. He had a daughter, Valiero had a son.
If these two could be married it would at once
bring the self-made Memmo into the charmed circle
of the aristocracy; and while Valiero should become free from debt, Memmo should rise to that
lofty world where dwelt those whose noble names
were inscribed in the Libro d' Oro.

Valiero came to him one day in want of more
money.

Memmo asked what security he had to give.

Valiero's property was all covered by mort-
gages, and nothing was left but his ships and cargoes.

" I have ships," said he, " with cargoes of silk
and spices. They will soon be here, and retrieve
all."

Memmo shook his head.

" A ship at sea is no security. The Turks, the
tempests, and all other accidents and dangers, await

them. Besides, you have been unfortunate, and my experience has been that when once ill luck assails a man, it never leaves him."

Valiero sighed.

"It's true," said he, "I've been unfortunate of late. But I have hope yet."

"Your last hope."

"It's my last hope."

"And if it fails?"

"Then I'm a ruined man," said Valiero.

"Ruined. O, no," said Memmo: "not ruined — not while I live. We'll pull through, after all."

Valiero looked at him earnestly, as though not quite understanding him.

"You mean that you will help me?" he asked.

"Well, I've got an idea," said Memmo. "I've been thinking over it for some time, and I may as well mention it now. You see our connection thus far has been of a purely business character."

"Yes," said Valiero.

"Well, we might place our connection upon a different footing."

"I don't think I understand you," said Valiero, with a look of surprise. He had not the slightest idea what Memmo's meaning could be.

"You have a son," continued Memmo.

"Yes," said Valiero, still in the same state of surprise.

"I have a daughter," said Memmo, and then hesitated.

"What of that?" said Valiero. "What has that to do with my business."

"This," said Memmo. "Listen. Ruin is before you, and poverty, and despair. You can never survive your fortunes. You have fallen too far. Now all this may be avoided by the marriage of your son with my daughter."

For a few moments Valiero stared in silence, as though unable to credit the proposal.

"Your daughter!" he said, at length. "My son! married! Why, man, are you mad?"

The tone with which Valiero spoke was worse than the words. It was the tone which might be assumed by some superior being. The prospect of ruin had not diminished Valiero's pride, and it was evident that he regarded Memmo's proposal with unutterable scorn and indignation, as a piece of unwarrantable insolence and presumption. Memmo said not a word, but the fierce passion within him made his heart throb fast and furious; and if he did not speak, it was because he found no words that could express his feelings.

"You don't understand," continued Valiero, with a laugh of scorn. "We nobles can meet ruin if it comes — and poverty — yes, and despair — for all these are sent by Providence, and there is nothing left but submission and brave endurance ; but to stoop to dishonor, to soil our family name, to damn our posterity by a mésalliance ! O, my good man ! is it possible that you have lived in Venice, and can make this proposal to a Valiero? Why, you're mad."

With these words, Valiero retired, leaving Memmo furious. The insult, the scorn, the abuse, all were intolerable. He had but one thought — vengeance. He would press his claims at once. He would crush Valiero in the dust. He would show no mercy, nor would he ever repeat the offer.

Memmo had been very confident in his maxim, that when ill luck fastens upon a man it never leaves him; but he was destined to find it untrue. For after all, though Valiero's difficulties had been great, still his resources were immense, and it was hardly possible that out of his vast wealth, which was afloat at sea, he should receive nothing. The fact was, he received it all. The ships had been delayed in various ways: but a few days after his interview with Memmo one of them arrived; and afterwards others came, arriving one by one, until at last all had reached port, bringing with them cargoes of immense value. Valiero's difficulties all vanished, and for the risk he had run he received corresponding profits.

All this sank deep into Memmo's soul. Valiero was now completely out of his power, and moreover far beyond his reach. Yet he still cherished his desire for vengeance, and resolved to watch with sleepless vigilance for some chance to gratify this desire. But first of all he sought out Valiero, and

made a most abject apology. With great apparent
frankness he owned up all. He said that he thought
him ruined—was resolved to help him—but at
the same time, from foolish fondness for his daughter, made the proposal. A common man like himself, he said, did not understand the feelings of the
nobility. For himself, he was only a plain and simple man, and if he had offended, it was uninten-
tional, and was only owing to foolish parental fondness. To all this Valiero listened most gracious-
ly. His prosperity made him condescending and
affable.

"Never mind," said he. "Say no more. I shall
only remember the help you gave me; and mark
you, Memmo, I believe you are an honest man, for
you did not charge half so much as you might."

"Heaven save me from taking usury," said
Memmo. "What profits I make I come by hon-
estly."

After this, Memmo was treated by Valiero with
much kindness and confidence. The explanation,
so humbly made, had smoothed away all difficulties,
and effaced every unpleasant recollection. The
business connection remained, although now it was
Memmo who appeared to solicit favors, and who
made all the advances. He was keeping Valiero
in view, and watching all his acts so as to find
something of which he might avail himself in his
efforts after revenge. At length his vigilance was
rewarded, for an event happened which was the
very thing that he desired.

There was a certain French noble, the Count de Ligny, with whom Valiero had formed a close friendship in early youth, when De Ligny had been on the ambassador's suite at Venice. Afterwards Valiero had visited France, and the two had kept up their friendship ever since. It happened that a conspiracy had been discovered by the French King Louis XI., in which De Ligny was implicated; but on receiving notice from his friends, the noble escaped the king's wrath, and fled from France. On reaching Italy, he sought refuge with his friend Valiero, at Venice. King Louis received information of this, and at once sent a demand to the Venetian government for the surrender of the fugitive. The Venetian government promised to make a search for him, and if he were in their dominions, to deliver him up, which promise came to the ears of Valiero, and made him anxious to send his friend out of danger.

Assistance was necessary in this matter, and no one seemed so well able to give the requisite help as the honest and simple Memmo. To Memmo, therefore, he applied; and that worthy, with the affectation of deep sympathy, promised to find a vessel and go himself with De Ligny to Ancona. Valiero was deeply grateful, and Memmo at once set out to provide the means of escape. The preparations were hurriedly made, and before twenty-four hours had passed, De Ligny was beyond the reach of danger. Memmo returned, and Valiero's gratitude could scarce find words.

That very day, Memmo dropped into the " Lion's Mouth " information against Valiero, for harboring the rebel De Ligny, and sending him away to Ancona, in spite of the Venetian government.

It was a serious charge. The Venetians were anxious, above all things, to keep on friendly terms with France, and had hoped very earnestly to be able to gratify this wish of King Louis. Valiero was therefore arrested, and his family was plunged into an abyss of despair. The loss of the head of that family was terrible, but beyond this there was a series of calamities — the torture of their loved father — the condemnation and degradation — the confiscation of his property — poverty, shame, and despair. All these calamities lowered before them, and crushed them into the dust. These same things were in the mind of Memmo, and in all the glow of gratified pride he exulted in his revenge, and had to seek out Valiero's family in order to feast his eyes upon their grief. The only one of the family whom he could see was Marco, the son of Valiero, the very one to whom he had once proposed to marry his daughter. The exultation of Memmo made him forget his usual caution; and Marco, who had at first expected to find sympathy, and perhaps the humble offer of assistance, was horrified at finding him transformed to an open enemy, whose coarse and brutal triumph was displayed without any attempt at concealment.

" Aha ! " he said; " so he's gone ! I've heard all

about it. Now he knows that a Venetian noble is not a god. Now he may know what it is to suffer degradation, and to feel what he has made me feel — shame, and humiliation, and despair."

"Of whom are you speaking?" asked Marco.

"Of your father," said Memmo; "your father in the *piombi.*"

The hot blood mounted to Marco's brow, but he repressed his feelings. For quick as thought there came into his mind a strange suspicion, which, when it had once come, grew stronger. Mastering, therefore, his emotion, he said in a slow and self-contained manner, —

"I was not aware that my father had done you wrong."

"Wrong! He did me outrageous wrong," said Memmo ; "wrongs never to be forgotten. Never shall I forgive him, as he stood with his haughty face, and crushed me into the dust."

"I thought you were his friend," said Marco, in the same tone.

"His friend!" said Memmo. "Ah! so you did; so did he; he thought me his friend, too; but no; I had my wrongs to avenge, and I was waiting for my opportunity."

"Wrongs!" said Marco. "What wrongs were they?"

Upon this, Memmo poured forth the whole story with astonishing volubility and passion, interrupting it with a running fire of exclamations and execrations. It was the first time that Marco had heard of this. He knew Memmo's daughter, and almost smiled at the thought of such a wife. For she was well known among the golden youth of Venice, especially those fast young men who did business with Memmo, and generally went by the nickname of the "Golden Fleece," perhaps because at her father's house they were fleeced out of their gold. But it was not the time for smiles. The "Golden Fleece" was soon forgotten. The dark suspicion which had occurred grew stronger and stronger, and every word of Memmo's only served to confirm it.

"If my father," said he, in a haughty tone, "had been so base as to consent to such a thing, he would have found that my consent had also to be obtained."

"Aha!" said Memmo; "is that so; and is that your way, my young Lord of Glory?"

"Peace!" said Marco. "Look here, old Memmo. I have let you have full swing, and now a word with you. Don't boast so much; don't talk about the Piazza; for, hark you, I know who took the Count de Ligny to Ancona!"

At this Memmo's face grew livid. He stared at Marco as though suddenly struck dumb. Then he said, in a faltering voice, —

"Who?"

"You," said Marco; "my father told me all."

"He — he — said — that he would tell no one," said Memmo, in a scarce audible voice.

"Of course; but he would naturally except me, for he never kept any secrets from me."

Memmo seemed utterly overwhelmed. He had confidently believed that the secret of De Ligny's escape was known only to himself and Valiero. He had thought that Valiero had kept it secret even from his own family. Of Marco he had never thought at all. He had seemed a shallow youth, intent only on fashion or pleasure. Now he made the appalling discovery that this Marco was his father over again—with a keener vision, a stronger nature, and a deeper purpose than that father had ever known; and that he had read his thoughts, and saw him through and through. In that young but stern face there seemed not a trace of mercy; and in looking upon it Memmo seemed to be reading his doom.

"O, my dear, O, my dear," he said, confusedly. "It was all a jest. I was your father's dear friend; it was all a jest; a jest, you know. Old Memmo must have his jest."

Marco turned away abruptly. Memmo called after him, and tried to detain him. In vain. Marco shook him off. Then Memmo went home with a sense of impending ruin that filled him with despair.

As for Marco, all was plain to him, and he hastened to do the only thing that was in his power. He hastened to the Ducal Palace, and there dropped into the Lion's Mouth his charge against Memmo.

Memmo was just beginning to rally from his first stupor of despair, and to think wildly of flight, when he was arrested by the awful messengers of the government. After this, but little remains to be told. On the rack the wretched Memmo revealed all. The government chose to consider him the more guilty. Valiero was set free, since his offence was the act of loyal friendship; but Memmo was punished, since his offence had been committed from the motives of avarice, jealousy, and treachery. Had he been a principal in the act, his property would have been confiscated; but as he was only an agent, the government contented themselves with imposing a fine which did not amount to more than nine tenths of all that he had. In addition to this, they banished him for life; and so Memmo, taking what little there was left, departed with the " Golden Fleece " to another and a kinder country.

After some conversation upon the incidents of the story, Vernon showed them another painting. This one was quite different from the last.

The scene was on the Piazza of St. Mark. The central figure was a young girl of exquisite beauty. This beauty was of a strange, Oriental cast, and was heightened by her costume, which was Turkish. Her beautiful face was full of mingled innocence and anxious eagerness; she seemed to be in search of something. A crowd was around her, who appeared to be trying by means of signs to communicate with the lovely stranger; but her eyes were fixed upon something in the distance, with a pathetic and wistful inquiry.

"You can make out nothing from that picture," said Vernon.

" I can," said Gracie.

" What is it ? "

" It tells its own story," said Gracie. "Your pictures speak, Mr. Vernon. This lovely Turk tells me that she has come to Venice in search of her lover: and here, amid all this crowd in the Piazza she is trying to find him."

Vernon looked at Gracie for a moment in silent admiration.

" I don't think," said he, " that I ever saw any one like you — in all my life — I wish — but no matter — shall I read the story ? "

" O, yes — do, by all means."

" It is the story of Fatima," said Vernon, who then went on and read from his manuscript.

CHAPTER XI.

The Story of Fatima.

ALFEO MANFRINI was the commander of a galley in the Venetian fleet that was despatched to the East with re-enforcements and supplies for the relief of the garrison at Scio. During the voyage a storm arose, and the fleet was scattered. When it had passed over, Manfrini found himself alone upon the deep, with not a single sail visible anywhere. He kept on his course, however, as before, hoping to fall in again with his friends, and at length saw sails in the distance, which he supposed to belong to the fleet that he was seeking. Towards this he hurried as fast as possible, and some of these, on seeing him, bore down upon him. But for Manfrini there was a dreadful disappointment. As the ships drew near, he perceived, to his horror, that they were not Venetian, but Turkish. He had flung himself into the midst of his worst enemies. To fight was not to be thought of, as that meant utter destruction; to fly was impossible, yet it was the only course open, and he tried it. The attempt, however, was all in vain. The enemy rapidly overhauled him, and at length he was captured.

He was conveyed to Constantinople, and after a time fell into the hands of a wealthy Turk who lived near Scutari. He was taken here by his new master, and found himself on an extensive estate, where there were many other slaves, over whom was an aged Turk of severe aspect and morose manner. The master left the whole management of the slaves to this overseer, whose name was Kaled, which said Kaled, after some examination of Manfrini, placed him in the garden to assist in the work that went on there. The work was not hard, and Kaled did not seem to expect much from the new slave; but Manfrini could not forget his beloved native land, and often and often the ground where he worked was wet with his tears.

Manfrini was left very much to himself. Kaled made the garden his peculiar care, and directed Manfrini about his daily task. It was the custom of Kaled, after his daily instructions, to retire, and leave Manfrini alone. The place to which his work was directed was a plot of ground immediately under the north end of the villa, and here Manfrini used to pass his time. There was a low basement with a window, over which was another window looking out upon him.

Here Manfrini was one day at work alone; and feeling weary, he sat down, and burying his face in his hands, began to weep. In the midst of his mournful thoughts and his wretched homesickness, his ear caught the sound of a low sigh. Hastily he looked up. There, at the window just above him, he saw a beautiful face. It was a young girl, and her large dark eyes were fixed upon him with earnest solicitude, while upon her sweet face there was an expression of tenderest sympathy. It was all taken in with a momentary glance, for no sooner had he looked up than the sweet face vanished.

Manfrini stood for some time staring at the window, half thinking that it was all a dream. The window there, open, without lattice, was now only a blank; yet a short time before it had been like a framework to the loveliest and sweetest face that ever his eyes had rested on. Who was she? Where had she gone? Would she ever come again? All thoughts of home, all feelings of homesickness, now fled away, and he could think of nothing but the lovely vision. He felt that it must be real. He could also guess who it might be. Old Kaled had muttered something about the lady Fatima, his master's daughter; and Manfrini had picked up enough of Turkish to understand common words. Fatima, the master's daughter! Was this Fatima? and did Fatima feel pity for him, the wretched captive? He longed to make some communication to her; to show her how sweet such pity was. But how? There was only one way — a harmless way, too. These flowers that grew around afforded a language of their own quite as intelligible as speech. Manfrini knew that language, and he had heard that it was invented in the East, in which case Fatima doubtless knew it as well as himself. So he gathered a small bunch which held these flowers — the Camellia Japonica, meaning " *My destiny is in your hands;* " the Cross of Jerusalem, " *Devotion:* " the Laurustine, " *I die if neglected;* " and the Pansy, " *Think of me.*"

This bunch he laid on the window, and then awaited the result.

Evening came, and he had to leave. He was full of curiosity as to how his little offering would be received, and full of recollections of that sweet vision. The next day came, and once more he was taken to the garden, and Kaled gave his directions and left. He now worked for some hours, keeping his eyes on the window, in hopes of seeing something. Nothing, however, appeared. He began to feel dejected. The lovely Fatima had not seen his offering, or had been offended. Such were his thoughts.

He was working under the window in a dejected mood, when suddenly a bunch of flowers fell immediately before him. He grasped it, and looked up. No one was there. He looked at the flowers. The first glance showed him that they formed an answer to his own offering.

They were these: The Snowdrop, "*Consolation;*" the Scarlet Ipomœa, " *I attach myself to you;* " and a spray of the Arbor Vitæ, " *Live for me.*"

Manfrini was now full of joy and hope. The lovely Fatima thought of him. Perhaps he might

see her again; perhaps the time might come when
he could speak to her. But for the present he
must content himself with the flowers. He now
made up another bunch, and placed it on the window.

One flower was the Lily of the Valley, "*My happiness has returned;*" another, the Sweet Sultan,
"*I rejoice;*" another, the Dahlia, "*I am thine forever;*" and to these he added the sweet little "*For-
get-me-not.*"

This bunch he placed on the window and waited;
but for some time there was no response, and he
had to console himself with those first flowers,
which he treasured next his heart.

At length one day, after Kaled had gone, Manfrini saw the well-remembered face. She smiled
sweetly and sadly, then vanished. This was something. It showed that she might come again. That
smile was like sunshine, and cheered Manfrini all
the day. At length towards evening, just before
his time for retiring, the face appeared again. He
started forward with clasped hands, in an attitude
of entreaty. This time the face did not vanish.

The window was low, and but a few inches above
Manfrini's head.

"O," he murmured, in his faltering Turkish, " do
not go; let me see you a moment."

A flush passed over the lovely face of Fatima,
and her eyes drooped, hidden under the long silken
fringe of eyelashes.

"Your face," said Manfrini, "is like sunlight. When you go, all is dark to me. Will you speak, and let me hear your sweet voice?"

"Alfeo!" said Fatima, in a low, timid voice. It was his Christian name — the name by which he was known here, for the Turks found it easier to pronounce than Manfrini.

"Fatima!" said Manfrini. He drew nearer. Her little hand was resting on the window-sill. He pressed it in his.

From that time forth not a day passed on which Manfrini did not see Fatima and speak to her. There was no one to watch them. Old Kaled seemed to have other things to attend to; and as for Fatima, she was able to elude any observation or suspicion within the household. Manfrini had a great motive now for mastering the Turkish language, and made rapid progress under so sweet a teacher.

"Are you happy here?" asked Fatima, one day.

"So long as I may hope to see you," said Manfrini, "I am happy. I want no more."

"But you are a slave," said Fatima. "In your own country you are a noble. If you embraced Islam you might be a noble here."

"Ah, yes," said Manfrini; "but that is impossible."

"Then you must escape," said Fatima.

"Escape!" said Manfrini; and at the thought a thrill of joy passed through him; but a moment after it was followed by despondency. "No, no," said he; "it is impossible. Besides, so long as you are here, this slavery is sweeter than liberty without you."

Tears started to Fatima's eyes. She smiled, and then said, in a low and tremulous voice, —

"If you could escape — would you?"

"And leave you!" said Manfrini, reproachfully.

"Would you take me?" whispered Fatima.

"O Heavens!" said Manfrini; "would you? Do you mean it? Could you give up your home, and incur the danger — the peril of flight?"

"I have been thinking of it," said Fatima, gently.

Manfrini seized her hand, and covered it with kisses.

"Listen," said Fatima. "I have been planning this ever since I first saw you. There is a fisherman here devoted to me. I have spoken with him. It is all arranged. So soon as you are ready to start, you can go."

At this Manfrini was again overwhelmed.

"Go! Escape!" he faltered. "But you! will you let me go? and do you think I can leave you?"

"You need not leave me," said Fatima, "if you will take me. And I am glad to hear you say that you do not want to leave me."

"Leave you!" said Manfrini. "To lose you would be worse than death. You have made me forget my country. You are all the world to me. I would rather be with you — a slave — than be free, if I had to lose you.   O, then, if you have the courage to do it, come with me; let us fly.   You shall be as rich and as honored as you are now, if we only escape: and all my life shall be spent in the effort to make you happy."

" I believe every word that you say," said Fatima, simply, " and your words are very sweet to me.   Yes, I will go, Alfeo; and for you I will give up father and mother, and country and friends, and religion, too, Alfeo.   I will give up all for you. And I have made all the arrangements.   And my father is away now, so that we can leave with less danger."

A long conversation followed, in which Fatima explained the whole plan which she had made. She had seen that Manfrini would remain a miserable slave till he died, nor could he ever be more than a slave to her, unless he could escape; but in his native land he would be rich and noble.   She had deliberately chosen to give up all for his sake, preferring by this venture to be his wife at Venice, rather than his master's daughter at Scutari.   She had bribed a fisherman, who was prepared to take them to the Morea, whence they could go to Venice; and for funds to support them on the way, she had her jewels.   Finally, immediate action was necessary, so as to leave before her father's return.   It was arranged, therefore, that they should leave on the following evening.   The fisherman should come for Manfrini, and Fatima would join them as soon as possible.

That night Manfrini could not sleep. Before him was the prospect of escape, of home, friends, honors, of Fatima. without whom all else would be poor indeed. Morning came, and he went to his work. Once or twice he saw Fatima's face at the window; but she only staid for a moment, and then, with a warning gesture, withdrew. Manfrini hoped to have the opportunity of speaking with her, but this was eclipsed by the greater hope of flying with her from these hostile shores.

Old Kaled that day did not leave at his usual time. On the contrary, he busied himself in the garden until dark. Once or twice Fatima appeared at the window, but she saw Kaled and retreated. Manfrini was troubled at this. It was unfortunate, and looked as though Kaled had done it intentionally. At length it was dark, and the old Turk came up to him.

"Follow me," said he, in his usual rough tone.

Manfrini was startled at this, and followed Kaled full of dark forebodings. The old Turk led the way, and went out into the road, and down towards the shore, which was not far away. Here there was a boat.

"Get in," said he, with an imperious gesture.

Manfrini did so, wondering what it all meant. His only thought was, that his project had been discovered, and that he was being taken away to death — that secret and terrible death by bowstring, with which the Turks were wont to punish those wretched slaves who had incurred their displeasure. A wild thought of resistance came to him : but he was unarmed, and Kaled was armed. He therefore obeyed in silence, yet in despair.

Kaled pushed off the boat, and taking the helm, ordered Manfrini to hoist the sail. Manfrini did so. The sail caught the favoring wind, and the boat, shooting out from the bay, went far away over the waters.

" Where are we going ?" asked Manfrini at last, unable to repress the impatience and anxiety with which he was tortured.

" Peace, slave," said Kaled, sternly, " and obey my commands."

Manfrini subsided into silence, and gave himself up to despairing thoughts. Yes, all was plain ; he had been discovered. The crafty Kaled had come to punish him, and was now taking him to death. As for Fatima, she was lost forever.

Hour after hour passed. Sleep was impossible. The stern Kaled sat as rigid as stone at the helm, and Manfrini's despairing thoughts of Fatima were intermingled with wondering conjectures as to his destination. It was with such feelings as these that he passed the night, for all that night the boat sped over the waves, borne by a favoring breeze ; and when the sun rose, Manfrini looked around, and saw nothing but a wide expanse of water, with low lines here and there on the horizon, marking the presence of distant shores.

Kaled pushed a box towards Manfrini.

"Eat," said he, pointing to the box.

Manfrini shook his head and turned away. He had reached the extreme verge of despair. Fatima was lost. This fierce old Turk had brought him for many a mile out into the sea. For what? For some fresh captivity? If that was so, he would not submit. Better a brief struggle here, even if he should perish, than a lingering captivity in Smyrna or Alexandria. To make a sudden spring upon that old man seemed an easy thing. True, he was armed, but he might be taken unawares.

"I think I will take some food," said Manfrini, quietly.

He drew nearer to Kaled, and as he opened the lid of the box, watched the old man with cautious sidelong glances. The Turk did not notice him. He was looking at vacancy with an abstracted face, — the face of one who was buried in his own thoughts, — and saw nothing of the world around.

Suddenly, with a bound, Manfrini had flung himself upon Kaled, with one hand on his throat, and the other on the pistol in his belt. The next instant Kaled lay on his back in the bottom of the boat, and Manfrini, with the muzzle of the pistol pressed against his forehead, cried, —

"Villain, I have you now! You must die! But tell me how you found out our plan; and tell me what has become of Fatima. If you wish to live,

11

speak the truth. If I detect one single lie, I will blow your brains out."

Kaled gasped for breath. Then he spoke, and as he spoke, every word thrilled through the inmost heart of Manfrini.

"O, signor, forgive me for what I have done. I am a Venetian. I am trying to escape."

These words were spoken in Italian with the Venetian accent, and at their sound the passion and the fury of Manfrini all passed away. Amazement overwhelmed him, and all his soul was moved to its inmost depths by the sound of that loved Italian speech, to which he had so long been a stranger. He started back. the pistol dropped from his hand. He raised the aged man with tender hands from the bottom of the boat, and in a voice which was tremulous with agitation, he gasped forth, —

"Who are you ?"

"I am your countryman. Forgive me," said the other.

"But you are a Turk — a Mohammedan."

"I will tell you all," said the old man, "and then kill me if you choose. Still, hear me first, and then do as you please. I am a Venetian," the old man began. "My name is Giuseppe Villano. Twenty years ago I was on my way in my own ship with a cargo of silk stuffs and spices from Rhodes to Venice, and was captured. I lost everything. I was taken to Beyrout, then to Damascus, and then to other places. You, who have been a captive, know something of what I felt; but my fate was harder than yours, for I fell in with cruel masters, and lived for three years in anguish and despair. The hope of returning to my native country left me. Such a thing seemed impossible. Then came the devil to me in my despair, and showed me how I might escape from my chains. I had only to say the Mohammedan formula; only to utter a half dozen words, and at once I might have all the rights of a free man.

"Enough. I will not dwell upon this. I abjured my God and my Saviour: I gave up my country; I became a renegado,—Kaled, the Turk,—and thus I have been for years. At first the change was pleasant. I was no longer beaten and tormented. I found employers readily, and had all the comforts that I could wish. But at last there occurred something which has embittered my whole life. It was a truce between the sultan and the doge. Prisoners were exchanged. Word came that all the Venetians should be set free, and sent home. I saw it all. I saw the Christian captives delivered from their captivity. I saw all the Venetian prisoners set forth for their home. All went. I — I alone could not go. I had sold myself to the devil. I had denied my God. I had given up my country, and this was my reward. O, young man, believe me, the devil is a hard master; and if we are captured again, beware of this temptation. Be

a slave in the galleys, go down into the deep dungeon; ay, kill yourself, do anything, commit any
crime, but do not give up your country, and deny
your God!

"As for me, I was condemned to eternal exile.
I might have escaped, but how could I go back to
Venice? My fellow-captives all knew what I had
done, and the devil had tempted them with my
example. Now I had given myself up to everlast-
ing infamy, and I had erected an eternal barrier
between me and my home.

"After the return of the Venetians, I became a
prey to homesickness, and for years that feeling
has never left me. I have suffered so much from
this that my old sufferings as a slave seem enviable. O, how often I have longed to be able to go
back to that happy, happy slavery, when my sufferings were only those of the body, and my mind
was at peace with God! Then, at least, I could
pray; but now — now — the heavens are all black
above me; and I have lived all these years without God and without hope in the world. At last
I found myself in Scutari. Here I determined to
take the first chance that presented itself, and go
home to Venice. But it was a time of war, and to
set forth on such a voyage was extremely difficult.
It was while I was thus deliberating over my best
course that you came. I at once resolved to win
your confidence, and get your assistance in my
plan. But in order to do this I should have to tell

you my story, and it was a hard thing to do. So I postponed it, and contented myself with securing you a pleasant position and kind treatment.

"A short time ago I was in the basement room, and heard your voice. I looked out, and saw you talking with some one. I heard you speak her name. I understood it all. Pardon me if I say that I listened. I listened then, and at other times, for all my fate seemed now bound up in you. To go home was my one thought — to go home, to see my country, to confess to my God. Then I could give myself up to the authorities; I could confess; I could spend all the rest of my life in prayer. O, to be able to pray once more! to pray! but now I dare not, nor shall I dare to pray till I have confessed my sins: till the church shall receive me back into her fold, all unworthy, yet penitent, and with a broken and a contrite heart, which the God of pity will not despise.

"Young man, do not think of me as a treacherous eavesdropper. O, think of me as a despairing sinner, seeking some way of escape from eternal death — a lost soul, with but one ray of hope, with but one last faint chance of flying back to Him whom I had denied.

"And so," continued the old man, after a pause, "I heard all, and took advantage of it. I took you away, and now take your vengeance. Kill me; you have the power. I will not resist. But remember it is not my life that you will destroy;

it is my immortal soul. Can you do that? Can you stand between a despairing wretch and his God? Can you stop my flight? Are you thinking of going back, in your despair, to see the one you love? I have read your face well. I see it all. But, O, for the love of Heaven, do not stop my flight. Help me to seek my soul's peace. Be pitiful. What is your earthly love compared with the eternal salvation of a fellow-creature? Let me but stand once more in Venice. Let me confess my sins. Let me once more, if it is but once, be able to look up to the God of mercy, and utter but one word of prayer."

The old man had told all his story in a wild and vehement manner, and with deep agitation. These last words were uttered in a voice of despairing entreaty, for Manfrini's stern face seemed to indicate a merciless soul. But Manfrini was not merciless. He had been profoundly moved by this confession, and his own sorrows seemed slight indeed compared with the anguish and the remorse of his companion.

"Say no more," said he. "Heaven forbid that I should stand between a penitent sinner and his God. For me, I have lost what is dearer than life; but you, I plainly see, have been thrown in my way by Heaven — by One who willeth not the death of a sinner, but that all should turn unto Him and live."

Manfrini said no more. He gave up the tiller

to Kaled, or rather Villano, and resumed his seat forward. After this they sailed on in silence. The breeze was fair. Once or twice they saw a sail in the distance, but they themselves were not seen, or not regarded. After two or three days, during which they had more than once a narrow escape from capture, they reached Candia. Here they found a ship which was just leaving for Venice; and embarking in this, they at length reached their destination. Here he parted with Villano, and saw him no more. He learned, however, long afterwards, that the renegade had made his peace with the church, had entered a monastery, and had spent the remainder of his life in the exercise of that lofty privilege of prayer, which, through long suffering, he had come to regard as the highest blessedness of man.

But to Manfrini his return home gave but little pleasure. His friends thronged around him, and welcomed him with tears of joy as one risen from the dead. They heard all his story, and all were full of admiration for the lovely infidel who had lightened the darkness of his captivity and prepared a way for his escape. But all this was as nothing. To Manfrini it seemed as though all the light of life had gone out. All now was sad, and flavorless, and dull. His thoughts never ceased to revert to those sweet days when he used to stand gazing at Fatima's face, and hear the soft tones of her voice, and catch the glance of her loving eyes.

Those were the brightest days of his life ; and freedom without her was worse than slavery with her.

A year passed away. Manfrini had found new occupations, yet his heart was unchanged, and Fatima's image was as clear and prominent as ever in his memory. The thought that she was lost to him forever was now a familiar one, and his only care was to trust to that mighty hand of Time which heals all things.

Such was the condition of Manfrini, when one day there landed at the Piazetta a foreign lady, richly dressed and of exquisite beauty. Her appearance in the thronged Piazza excited universal attention, for even there, where many nations and many faces were always represented, there never had been seen any one like this. What was more extraordinary was her eager glance of inquiry. She traversed the whole Piazza many times, and then began to question passers by. It was evident that she was seeking some one. But all that she could say was, —

" Alfeo ! "

Alfeo ! And who or what might Alfeo be ? Alfeo was a common enough name, like Matteo, or Taddeo, or Tito, or Giuglio, or Lorenzo. It was indeed a wonderful thing that a beautiful stranger should come alone to the Piazza di San Marco, and seek after some one of whom she knew nothing more than that he was named " Alfeo."

Yet still the beautiful stranger went about, asking with plaintive tones and anxious looks after " Alfeo."

Many were the conjectures that were made. Some thought that she was a Candiote, who had lost her father, and was trying to find him ; others, that Alfeo was her attendant : others again thought that she was insane, and had escaped from her keepers. A thousand other conjectures were made : but all were at length cut short by the appearance of the agents of the Ten, who swooped down upon the beautiful stranger, and bore her away.

After that every one grew as silent as the grave, and talked of everything else under the sun.

Very fortunate was it for the beautiful stranger that she had come to Venice, for there the government, with its countless eyes and innumerable spies, knew all the movements of all the people. The story of Manfrini was well known to them. Interpreters soon enabled them to learn the story of the stranger.

She was Fatima, the daughter of Almamun, the Kadi of Scutari. She had fled from home, and came to Venice to find Alfeo. This Alfeo was a Venetian who had been a slave, and with whom she had intended to fly : but he had by some mistake gone away with the overseer. So she had waited for a chance to follow, and had come over the sea, braving a thousand perils, in perfect faith and touching innocence, never doubting that she would find her dear Alfeo here.

The agents of the Ten did not leave the beautiful stranger long in suspense. They knew who this Alfeo was, and at once sent for him. He came with all that trepidation which such a message might excite in a Venetian breast. He entered the hall with a dark and grisly horror in his soul, with thoughts of the rack and the wheel.

The first thing that he saw was Fatima! And she — the little innocent, all regardless of the terrors of the Inquisition, and the Bridge of Sighs, and the Council of Ten — no sooner saw him than with a great cry of joy she rushed into his arms.

Here Vernon ended.

"Well," said Gracie.

"Well," said Vernon.

"Is that all?" she asked.

"Why, of course."

"But you have not finished it."

"How?"

"Why, you should have told all about their marriage."

"Why? Isn't that all understood? Of course they were married, and of course they lived happily ever after. That is all implied in the termination of the story. Why should it be expressed?"

"O, yes," said Gracie, "you're right. It is your art, and you scorn to say things openly when they can be suggested. I take back my objection, and see that your way of ending the story is best. But,

then, you know one loves to have everything plainly stated ; and that's the way the old story-tellers
always did, for they always made it a point of conscience to end a story with a minute description of
the wedding ceremony."

" I'm glad you made that criticism," said Vernon,
after a pause. " I see that I've depended too much
on suggestions. After this I will be more out-
spoken."

Shortly after they all retired for the night.

CHAPTER XII.

Uncle Moses still on the Search. — On to Venice. — The Hotel Zeno. — Distressing Disappointment. — A Visit to the Venetian Police. — Frank and Bob go the Rounds. — A wonderful City. — Lost.

WE left Uncle Moses last at Padua. Further conversation with the landlord elicited the information that he had recommended the Hotel Zeno to David and Clive. This was encouraging, for it seemed likely that the boys would go there, and that they might be found at that place: or that, at least, some information might be gained about them. But their only plan was to hurry onward as fast as possible, so as to catch these volatile lads before they might leave for some new place. Accordingly they left Padua on the following morning, and in due time reached Venice.

Arriving here, they found themselves in the midst of wonders which impressed them as they had impressed Clive and David. This strange silent city, with canals for streets, with boats for carriages, with no sound of life, with universal stillness broken only by the ringing of bells or the cry of gondoliers, — it never fails to fill the mind of the new comer with wonder and admiration.

But Uncle Moses was altogether too anxious to give way to feelings like these, and Frank and Bob, though full of the excitement of youth, felt themselves somewhat restrained by the sympathy which they had for the sorrows of their aged relative. And so they were all impatient to reach the Hotel Zeno, so as to learn what might now be in store for them. Until the lost boys should be found, there could be no peace for Uncle Moses, and consequently no pleasure for Frank and Bob.

The gondola brought them to the Hotel Zeno, and here they made inquiries. Uncle Moses, in his deep despondency, was prepared for some fresh disappointment, and therefore it only elicited a new though somewhat deeper groan when he heard the reply to Frank's eager question. He heard the same news that had already mocked him at Bologna, Ferrara, and Padua — the same news which he had expected and dreaded to hear at Venice.

Those boys were here. O, yes: it was yesterday morning they came with a young lady — a Miss Lee.

This piece of information was simply overwhelming. A young lady! Miss Lee! What did this mean? Were these brats of boys beginning to pay attentions to young ladies? Were they infatuated? Was it Clive, or David, or both? Frank and Bob stared at one another in utter bewilderment.

Then, of course, came the usual information that they had gone away.

"Where?" was the anxious question.

They did not know.

Frank now thought of asking this Miss Lee about them, and inquired after her.

The answer was, that she had gone away, too; and what was more, that she and the boys had all gone away together. Nothing more than this were they able to say. They had not noticed the movements of the boys, or of Miss Lee, very particularly; but one of the servants mentioned that there were a gentleman and a lady who seemed to be with them.

"A gentleman and a lady!" said Frank, who caught at this. "Do you know their names?"

They did not.

"A gentleman and a lady. Friends of Miss Lee, no doubt, and therefore probably English or American. The fact is, Uncle Moses, Dave and Clive have got among some pleasant acquaintances, and have left the place to go with them."

"But where?" cried Uncle Moses. "Where?"

"And echo answers, 'Where?'" said Bob.

"Where have they gone?" cried Uncle Moses, who was now quite beside himself with grief and anxiety. "What are they thinking of? What do they mean? They can't keep this up long. Even if they want to leave me, they can't leave me always. They haven't enough money to last them over a week at the furthest. Why haven't they left some message? O, boys! boys! I tell you what it is, I'm afraid — I'm afraid — I'm dreadful afraid."

"Afraid of what?" asked Frank.

"That somethin's happened," wailed Uncle Moses. "It's a dreadful place. I've been dreadful afraid of Vee-nice all my life, but I never had an idee of how bad it was before. Why, there's nothin' but water, an' a person can't go three steps without danger of gettin' drownded. An' then the spies! O, dear, who knows but that this Miss Lee is some spy in the pay of the Council of Ten? and this lady and gentleman, that they speak of, who knows but that they are the agents of the Inquisition!"

"Nonsense, Uncle Moses!" said Frank, with a laugh. "They don't have these things in Venice now. This is a free country."

"A free country!" exclaimed Uncle Moses. "I only wish I was well out of it; an' when I get the poor lost boys back again, I know I won't stay here much longer."

"O, well," said Frank, "it's a comfort to know that they are in this place. We shall find them soon enough, I dare say."

"But how do I know that they're in Venice at all?" said Uncle Moses, despairingly. "They may have taken the steamer for Jerusalem, or Jericho, or the North Pole!"

Uncle Moses was greatly agitated. Frank did not try to argue with him. He merely persuaded him to go to his room and take rest.

"This is a good place to stop at," said he. "You lie down and try to sleep. Bob and I will go to the police office, and get them to make inquiries after David and Clive. We'll ask if they know anything about this Miss Lee. We'll go about the city, too, in the boat, and keep our eyes wide open, and perhaps we may find them. So you try, Uncle Moses, to get a little sleep, and don't fret yourself more than you can help."

This, however, Uncle Moses refused to do. He was not willing to let them go, especially when their journey led them into the midst of those formidable powers of darkness — the Venetian police. Dread indeed was the necessity which lay upon them to make such a visit, yet since it had to be done, Uncle Moses determined to go with them.

The Bureau of Police was in an edifice close by the Piazza of St. Mark's; and it is a singular thing, that while David and Clive were in the cathedral with Vernon and Gracie, the anxious Uncle Moses, with Frank and Bob, were at that very time in the police building — so near were they to a meeting.

Their business was stated as briefly as possible. They explained how David and Clive had gone away from them, and how they had come in search of them, and had finally lost them at the Hotel Zeno. The official, with whom they were communicating, could "spik Ingelis," but was apt to make blunders here and there. He promised to do all that could be done to find them, and took down their address so as to communicate with them upon learning anything of the lost boys.

Frank now thought of something that might be of assistance in the search.

"The people of the Hotel Zeno tell me," said he, "that the boys went away in company with a lady named Miss Lee."

The official seemed struck by this.

"Missa Lee," said he, and then turned over the leaves of a big book before him.

"Missa Lee," said he again, in a thoughtful voice. "Af she been in Venezia?"

"Why, the boys left the Hotel Zeno along with her."

"Ah — alonga wis her. Den — she mus be in Verona."

"Verona!" cried Frank, in horror. He did not like the idea of setting forth on a new search, and leaving Venice almost the moment after his arrival.

"Si, si, Verona," said the official. "Dere is a Missa Lee in Verona. De popolo come to see about er. We af sent a messager after her."

"O, you've sent a message after her — have you?" asked Frank; "and did she go to Verona?"

"O, yis, si, she go to Verona. De amico — de frien — came ere to af a messager sent for Missa Lee at Verona."

"When was that?" asked Frank, eagerly.

"Yesterday."

"Then she must have left yesterday, and gone to Verona."

"I tink so," said the official, solemnly.

Now, this official was not the one with whom Vernon had spoken, and knew nothing at all about this affair; that is, nothing more than the fact that the aid of the police had been asked in order to find a Miss Lee at Verona. Now, as this new party came to ask the aid of the police in a new search, and also mentioned Miss Lee, the official very naturally thought that it was the same person; and so he judged from Frank's story that somehow there was a Miss Lee who had run away from her friends, taking with her the two boys.

"Dey are too young," said the official; "too young to run away, an what does she want wit two of dem?"

At this Frank and Bob both laughed; but poor Uncle Moses looked more distressed than ever. There seemed no end to his troubles now.

"O, nevare minda," said the official, who noticed the troubled face of Uncle Moses, and seemed to feel pity for him: "nevare mind; we sall send ar de messager, an we sall findar dem all. Missa Lee, when she come back she bring dem."

" When did you send the message to Miss Lee ? "
asked Frank.

" Dis morning."

" And when do you expect to hear about her ? "

" O, to-day or to-morrow. It cannot be vera
long time : dat is, if she is in Verona ; if not, why,
dat is different."

" At any rate," said Frank, consolingly, to Uncle
Moses, " at any rate they can't be far away. Verona is only a little beyond Padua."

" O, that's the way it allers is," said Uncle Moses : " they're allers ony jest a little distance off ;
but what's the good of that to me, when I never
can lay my hand on them ? "

The official promised to do everything in his
power to find the boys, and as there was a possibility of their being in Venice, he promised to
have inquiries made at the hotels and lodging-
houses. Frank promised to come again in the evening, and then, with many thanks for the civility
which he had shown, they took leave of the re-
spectable official, and returned to the Hotel Zeno.

They now persuaded Uncle Moses to lie down,
and try to obtain some rest and sleep. Poor old
Uncle Moses was by this time quite worn out with
anxiety and fatigue, so that he did not seem to have
much mind of his own about anything. He yielded
to their persuasion, and when Frank informed him
that he and Bob were going to look about the city,
and suggested the possibility of meeting with the
boys, he made no objection.

Frank and Bob now went down and engaged a gondola. But they thought it too stupid to be rowed around by a dull gondolier, and it seemed to them to be far better fun to have the boat all to themselves, and go wherever the whim might guide them. Had Uncle Moses been present, he would certainly have objected to this; but as he was not present, the two did as they chose. They had no difficulty whatever in getting the exclusive use of the gondola, but the gondolier explained that they must stand up and push at the oars, and not sit down and pull them. For this is the custom of Venice, and indeed it is the only mode allowable in a populous city, where boats are continually passing and re-passing, when obstacles of every kind have to be guarded against, and sharp corners turned, and a constant lookout ahead maintained.

They rowed away up the Grand Canal, until at length they came to the Rialto. Here a vast bridge sprang across, with one wide arch, a marvel of mingled beauty and strength. There was a busy scene, for gondolas were passing to and fro, and there was something like noise from the shouts and cries of people afloat and ashore. They waited for some time looking upon the scene.

"There's something rather pleasant in this racket," said Bob. "Venice seems like a graveyard, it's so still. I shouldn't like to live here, but it would be a nice place to die in."

After passing the Rialto, they rowed on a little

farther, when the idea occurred to them of seeing
more of the interior of the city. So they turned
off to the right, and went down a long, straight
street. The houses here were much dilapidated,
yet they showed the traces of better days; and
some looked as though they might have belonged
to one of those merchant princes who formed the
Venetian nobility. On the whole, however, the
impression which they received was a sad one;
and it was with a feeling of relief that they at
length emerged from the street, and found themselves on the outskirts of the city, with a broad
expanse of water extending before them. Here
they rowed about for a while, and then, entering
another street, plunged into the heart of the city.

The streets here presented more variety. They
saw houses of all kinds — the mean, the splendid,
the simple, the pretentious. They passed by stately
churches, lofty towers, ponderous walls, and busy
squares. They went about quite at random, without caring where, and in the interest naturally
arising from such novel scenes, they were quite
unconscious of the lapse of time, until at length
Frank happened to look at his watch, and found
that it was six o'clock.

They now sought to return home, and found
themselves quite at a loss as to the proper course
to take. They rowed for a while in what seemed
the right direction, but only to find themselves
brought up at last at a point where a number of

narrow canals all united. They therefore turned and rowed back; but after a time they came to another place just like the last. Here they stopped, and once more considered their situation.

The fact is, they were utterly lost. Worse, it was now late, and growing later every moment. The boats that they met were but few in number. They could not see any one of whom they might ask the way.

At last they turned in desperation, and rowed up a wide canal, which seemed likely to lead somewhere. For a half an hour they went along, and at length, to their intense chagrin, they found themselves once more stopped in precisely the same way as before. There was now nothing else to do than to turn in some new direction.

Once or twice they met a gondola, and cried out,—

"Dov 'e la Piazza di San Marco?"

An answer was given, but it was in the Venetian dialect, and utterly incomprehensible.

Then they asked,—

"Dov 'e 'l Gran Canale?"

Another answer came, which was equally unintelligible.

At this time it was growing later. Darkness came on. Fortunately, the moon was shining, or else they would have been unable to go any farther. Even with the moonlight, the tall houses cast down heavy shadows, which made their way dark indeed. Had it not been for Uncle Moses, they would have considered this as a rare adventure. If they had been alone in Venice, with only themselves to think of, they would have enjoyed the situation, and, if the worst came to the worst, slept in the gondola all night, in its little cabin, on the soft cushions. But all the time they knew that Uncle Moses was waiting for them in new terror, and in deeper anxiety than ever.

At length they were fortunate enough to meet with a gondola which was disengaged. They succeeded in making known their wants to the gondolier, who took them in tow, and brought them at last to the Hotel Zeno.

It was about ten o'clock. They found poor Uncle Moses half frantic with anxiety, and filling the hotel with his wild lamentations. He received them as though they had been raised from the dead.

CHAPTER XIII.

The early Bird catches the Worm. — Bob's early Rising, and what came of it. — A Bath in the Grand Canal. — The Approach of the Enemy. — Flight and Pursuit. — The Dungeons of Venice.

FRANK had promised to call at the Police Bureau to find out what they had learned during the day; but he had forgotten all about this, and his careless wanderings through Venice had resulted in detaining him till this late hour. After the first joy which Uncle Moses felt at meeting with them again, he asked anxiously whether they had seen or heard anything of the lost ones.

"Nothing," said Frank. "I was in hopes that you might have heard."

At this Uncle Moses plunged down once more into the depths of gloom. Frank, as usual, endeavored to console him by trying to make him look on the bright side, and by promising to call upon the police early the next day.

Early on the following day, at about six o'clock, Bob was up, teasing Frank to go and take a swim. This was a pastime of which Bob was very fond;

but Frank did not share his enthusiasm, and on the present occasion cared for nothing except his sleep. So he rolled over in the bed, and merely remarked, —

"O, bother!"

Bob therefore decided to go alone; and, setting forth in rather scant clothing, he went down stairs. The door was unlocked; he passed out, and in a few moments he had divested himself of the little clothing which had covered him. Then he stood for an instant and looked at the canal beneath, and then raising his arms, he took a header straight into the turbid wave.

Rising, he struck out and swam towards the other side of the canal. This he reached, and then he started to return.

But when he was about half way across on his homeward journey, he heard a sound which made him instinctively turn his head. As he looked he saw a sight which filled him with a general sense of consternation. For he saw a boat which contained several men in police uniform, and these men all had their eyes fixed upon him; and what was worst of all, the police boat was coming straight towards him.

The only thing that he could do was, of course, to try to get back as soon as possible. And this he did. He struck out most vigorously. Terror lent him strength. He had never dreamed of anything illegal being in a harmless bath, but the looks of the policemen were enough to show him that his offence was serious. And so he struck out for dear life, hoping to escape. But, alas! he was distant from the Hotel Zeno, and the boat was near, and it could move much more quickly than he. The water foamed around him and behind him: yet still that terrible police boat kept on his track, and gained on him rapidly. At last, just as he reached the middle of the Grand Canal, he found that the police boat was close behind him. He struck out wildly, but it was of no use. The next instant the police boat was beside him, and a strong hand had seized him by the hair.

As Bob felt the grasp of the hand on his hair, he tried to dive. The movement was an unexpected one, and thus Bob jerked himself from the clutches of the policeman; then swimming under the boat, he came up on the other side, and again struck out for the hotel. He was discovered at once, and the boat pursued. By this manœuvre he had gained but little; still, the gain was something, and Bob was desperate. But the boat was close behind him, and once more Bob dived, and came to the surface in a new direction. This occurred two or three times; but the police followed all the more resolutely, and Bob was out of breath with his exertions. At last, as the boat came up to him once more, he found himself seized; and he was so utterly exhausted that he could not free himself. He had to cling to the boat for support.

There were four policemen in the boat, who regarded him with very stern faces. One of them said something to him in Italian, which, of course, Bob did not understand.

"Really," said he, "I am quite mortified, but I don't understand a word of what you are saying."

This was unintelligible to the police. They tried again with French, but with the same result. Then they spoke to him in German, but this also was a failure.

"He must be English," they said, "or Russian."

Bob's position was now far from pleasant. While dashing about in the freedom of nature, he had found the water highly enjoyable; but it was a far different thing to be floating in it, held by the hair, as a miserable captive. At that moment he understood perfectly the sorrows of the captured trout, the hooked salmon, the speared eel, or the netted shad. "You might as well have a hook in your gills," said he, afterwards, "as a hand clutching your hair." He was too sensible, however, and also too much exhausted, to make any struggle. He awaited the action of his captors, trusting that the future would afford some opportunity of escape.

His captors, on their part, did not know what to do exactly. The lad was a foreigner, and might possibly be a person of importance. This thing might have been done through ignorance, and even his fierce efforts to escape seemed natural. At the same time, the police mind is slow to admit the justice of release when one has been arrested, and in Venice old associations are still powerful.

They therefore had no idea of letting him go; yet at the same time they did not know how to get him into the boat. He was a foreigner, and might be some distinguished youth. They did not want to run the risk of offering unnecessary insult to one who might be, perhaps, an English milor, or a Russian prince. Prince, milor, or beggar, he might be any one of these, for he floated there in the water just as nature made him, and without any adventitious surroundings.

At last Bob made some signs which plainly intimated that he wished to clothe himself. He then pointed to the Hotel Zeno. The quick-witted Italians, who, of all men, are perhaps the most ready in the comprehension of the language of gesture, at once caught his meaning, and were very glad to comply with the request; for they did not care about taking away a naked prisoner, and besides they thought that the prisoner's clothes would give some general idea of his rank in life. So the boat moved slowly along towards the hotel, and Bob moved slowly after it, looking eagerly forward in the hope of seeing Frank. But no one was there. All was still, and not a soul seemed to be stirring. At length they reached the place where the steps ran down into the water. On the lower steps stood Bob, up to his waist in water, and made gestures to signify that his clothes were up there behind the door. The Italians understood him, and one of them got out upon the steps. The sight of this movement filled poor Bob with dismay. He had hoped that he should be allowed to go after his clothes alone; but the police, after having had so much trouble in capturing him, were by no means inclined to let him slip out of their hands so easily as that. So the one who had got out of the boat now took him from the hands of Bob's first captor and led him to the door.

Just inside of this were Bob's clothes. There was here a spacious vestibule, and the inner door was shut. The officer stood grimly waiting. Bob looked all around. Had the inner door been open, he would certainly have made a rush for liberty; but as it was, he saw that it was impossible.

One hope yet remained. He tried by signs to induce the officer to let him go into the hotel and communicate with his friends. But this the officer positively refused. The fact is, he began to think that Bob was not a prince in disguise; for the clothes that he put on were by no means suggestive of lofty rank or station. A pair of well-worn trousers and a night shirt constituted the simple attire in which Bob had come down to take his morning bath; and as he put these on he appeared to the police like some very insignificant lad, with whom they might be severe in safety.

In an American or English city the police would

certainly have granted so small a favor as this
which Bob requested; but all over the continent
of Europe there is far more rigor in the administration of affairs than is known in English-speaking
countries; and though Venice had long ago seen
the last of the Council of Ten, and felt no more
the stress of Austrian tyranny, still the influence
of the past remained, and the old habit of severity
was not laid aside. So the end of it all was, that
Bob was carried away captive.

CHAPTER XIV.

*Another lost Boy. — Terror and Despair of Uncle Moses. —
A wild Search. — Another Visit to the Police. — New Disappointment. — The End of it all.*

FRANK had rolled over again in bed, and
gone to sleep. It was later than usual
when he awoke. After dressing, he went
down to breakfast, and found Uncle Moses looking
more distressed than ever.

"We must hurry to the police office," said he.
"Don't be long over your breakfast. They must
have heard by this time of David and Clive."

"O, I'll only be a moment," said Frank.

"Where's Bob?"

"Bob!" repeated Frank.

"Yes."

"Bob! Why, he must be about somewhere.
Hasn't he had his breakfast yet?"

"Not that I know of."

"Why, haven't you seen him?"

"Seen him? No."

At this Frank stared, and began to feel troubled.
As for Uncle Moses, a look of deadly terror came
over his face.

"Where is he?" he gasped.

"I don't know," said Frank.

"You must have seen him. Did you see him when he got up?"

"O, yes. He ran out — to take a swim in the canal. He wanted — "

"A swim!" gasped Uncle Moses. "A swim in the canal!"

"Why, what of that?" said Frank. "He can swim like a duck. He wanted me to go with him, but I was too sleepy."

Uncle Moses sank into a seat, and there seemed no more life left in him.

"A swim in the canal!" he murmured. "He can swim! O, yes; but, then, this is no place. Who knows — who knows but that there may be sharks here — sharks, or devil fishes, or cuttle fishes, or sea sarpints? O, dear, dear! I do wish I was dead! O, Bobby, Bobby! has it come to this?"

Thus far Frank had never failed to find some words of comfort and consolation for Uncle Moses; but now he could find nothing to say. He himself was troubled. It seemed, indeed, very much as if some accident might have happened. There was the one, great, dark, undeniable fact, that Bob had gone off early in the morning to swim in the canal, and had not returned. Without a word Frank turned away, and went back to the room to see if there were any signs of a return from that bath.

One look filled him with dismay. There in a chair he saw Bob's clothes — the clothes which he usually wore through the day. Frank remembered now that Bob had hastily drawn on an old pair of trousers, and had rushed down in his night-shirt. The truth was plain. He had gone out to swim, and had not come back.

One thing yet remained. He must have stripped himself. Where were his clothes? That would decide the matter. Half frantic, he rushed down again, and out to the door. He looked all around, and it was with a feeling of relief that he found no signs of the clothes. Then he went to the landlord, and told him his fears. Had the servants found any clothes lying on the edge of the canal, or anywhere about? The landlord had inquiries made at once, but no one had seen anything of the sort. This was a relief to Frank: yet, after all, it was only a partial one. For the thought came to him that Bob might have gone somewhere else to take his bath, and that he would not have ventured to undress in such a public place as this. And yet where could he have gone? It was impossible to conjecture. What to do he knew not. He began to fear the worst. He knew that Bob was a good swimmer, but the suggestion of Uncle Moses about sharks was terrible, and produced an effect which was not to be shaken off. He was at his wits' end. He did not know what to do. A terrible dread was in his heart. The landlord could give him no consolation, for, indeed, he himself, and all the hotel people, who by this time had heard the news, had a certain solemn and awe-struck expression on their faces, which showed plainly that they, too, believed the very worst.

"You can do nothing," said the landlord, "and we can do nothing. You must go to the police. They will make inquiries; and the sooner you go the better."

It was the very thought that had already occurred to Frank, and he prepared to set forth at once. He hesitated for a while whether to take Uncle Moses, or leave him and go alone. At length he decided that it would be better to take Uncle Moses with him. When he came to his despairing relative with his statement, he received no answer except a heart-broken look, and Uncle Moses prepared in silence to accompany him. Then Frank informed the landlord of his intention, and begged him to do what he could during his absence towards searching after the missing boy. The landlord promised very earnestly to do whatever he could.

They now took a gondola, and went to the police station. Neither of them could speak a word. The thoughts of Uncle Moses were too deep for utterance. He was beyond the reach of sympathy, nor did he seek for any encouragement to hope. He had made up his mind for the worst. As for Frank, he, too, dreaded the worst, and did not attempt any longer to console his uncle with assurances which might in a short time prove altogether vain. Before long all would be decided, and until then Frank could only wait in silence.

At length they reached the Bureau of Police. They had to wait for some time, for no one was there who could speak English; but at length the official returned with whom they had talked on the former occasion. He greeted them very civilly.

"O, an so you af come," he said, "to see about de young boys. I sall look, an find if de messager haf come."

He went away, and was absent for some time. At length he returned.

"I am ver sorra," said he, "but notings haf come back from de messager."

Frank in his deep gloom hardly expected anything else; and so, after a short pause, he proceeded to state the cause of their present visit. The official listened most attentively.

When Frank ceased, he shook his head.

"It is vera infortnat," said he. "Dere is danger in de canale. I nevare go dere mysef; dere is too mooch danger. Bot I sall do all I can. I sall senda de men to investigare immediatemente. O, yes, I sall do all I can."

Some further conversation followed, and then they went back slowly and sadly to the hotel. They themselves could now do nothing. They could only wait, and hope to hear; but even this hope was faint. The police would go on the search,

but who could tell how long it would be before anything could be known? Indeed, their chief fear
now was, that nothing might ever be known, and
that Bob was lost forever. The loss of Clive and
David was nothing to this. They had been heard
of over and over again, but Bob had departed, and
had left no trace.

The long hours of the morning thus passed, and
midday came. With midday came also a strange
and startling message. It was from the Police
Bureau, and informed them that a boy had that
morning been arrested for swimming in the Grand
Canal, and that they were requested to come and
see if he was the one whom they sought.

In an instant the dark cloud of anguish rolled
away from the despairing minds of Uncle Moses
and Frank. They understood it all. Yet they
wondered why the official had not told them when
they made their inquiries. Perhaps he did not
know. That seemed the most probable conjecture.
At any rate there was no time to be lost; and so
they hurried to a gondola, and before long were
once more in the police station. There they met
with their friend, the official, who could " spik
Ingelis."

He informed them that he did not know, on their
former visit, of the arrest of any one for swimming,
but that since then he had learned the facts. He
had seen the prisoner, and had recognized him.

Upon this, Frank eagerly demanded his release.

The official said something about a violation of the law, and seemed to be in a very singular state of hesitation. He seemed to hint at a prolonged imprisonment for Bob, and said something about fines and money payments. As he touched upon this, he looked at Frank with a very peculiar expression.

Frank's intelligence caught at once at his meaning. In England or America he would not have thought it possible, but in Italy he had seen many things which showed him that a large number of the officials are not above receiving presents from those who wish their good offices. In this there was something which was very shocking to Frank's sense of propriety; but, then, too much was at stake for him to hesitate a moment. Bob in confinement, Uncle Moses breaking his heart — these were dread facts which had to be faced. With a hurried gesture, therefore, he placed his purse in the hands of the official, saying, —

"Get an advocate. Let us see him as soon as possible. There's enough there to pay any ordinary fine. And couldn't you free him first, and let the fine be settled afterwards?"

The hands of the official closed over Frank's purse with an eager grasp, which showed how welcome this offering was. His face beamed with benevolence, and his whole manner changed from official formality to one of sympathy and geniality.

"I sall see," said he. "Wait you; I not be long."

He departed, and they waited. They were not kept long. In less than ten minutes the door opened, and the official returned with the aspect of a kind benefactor, ushering in no less a personage than Bob himself. He had rather a sheepish look, and his somewhat scant attire made him have rather a disreputable appearance, but neither Uncle Moses nor Frank thought of that. They rushed upon him, and caught him in their arms, and almost wrung his hands off. As for Bob, he was amazed at these signs of feeling; but he bore it philosophically, and as soon as he could speak, he asked them if they had found Clive and David.

" No," said Frank ; " we've forgotten all about Clive and David. We've only been thinking of you. And mark you, my lad; this is the last time that you go in swimming."

" Well, to tell the truth," said Bob, " I think I shall postpone my next swim till I get home again. At the same time I must say it's rather hard treatment; and yet there are people who say that Italy's a free country. I rather think that the only liberty Italians know is the liberties they take with unoffending travellers."

Neither Uncle Moses nor Frank felt inclined to talk just here: so they hurried back with Bob as fast as possible to the hotel, and here they gained from him an account of his adventures. Of course the whole thing was now quite intelligible, and they saw that no blame could attach to poor Bob.

The recovery of Bob had produced one effect so important and so beneficial, that it made his little adventure seem like a very fortunate occurrence. That effect was produced upon Uncle Moses. Until then he had been sinking deeper and deeper into an abyss of gloom which was tending towards utter despair. Frank had already seen with deep concern the misery and prostration of the sorrowing old man, and feared that if it lasted much longer he would sink under his anxiety. The loss of Bob had been the final blow. He had scarcely been able to drag himself to the boat and into the police office. While there he had not been able to say one word, but had sunk into a seat, with his eyes staring fixedly upon the official. Then, returning to his hotel, he had passed the long hours of suspense like one demented. The news from the police had roused him; the final visit and the meeting with Bob had altogether overwhelmed him. In that great revulsion of feeling which had ensued, he had passed at one bound from the darkest despair to the highest and most exquisite happiness. On gaining Bob, he seemed to have gained everything; and from this he drew the strongest encouragement for the future. He now felt a calm assurance that David and Clive were all safe, — where, he did not know; yet still they were safe, and as he had recovered Bob, so he should recover them.

He was now his ancient and original self, as

talkative, as amiable, and as full of resources as ever.

"My mind's made up, boys," said he, as they sat in their room after luncheon. "I ben a thinkin' of it ever sence we found Bob. We must leave Venice."

"Leave Venice!" exclaimed both the boys, in mournful chorus. This announcement filled them with disappointment and dismay. "Leave Venice!" they repeated. "What! and give up our search for Clive and David?"

"Clive and David," said Uncle Moses, shaking his head; "they ain't here. It's no use a goin' an' a wastin' time in a place like this. You know they ain't here at all."

The boys had nothing to say to this.

"Besides, I can't stay here any longer. It seems like a dungeon. It was bad enough at first, but now, sence they've ben an' gone an' arrested a in-nocent child like Bob, why, I can't feel safe for a moment. We'll all be arrested next, an' if we air, why, we won't get off so easy as Bob did. The fact is, this here city is all honeycombed with dungeons; thar air spies everywhere; the Council of Ten is as bad as ever, and the Inquisition is in full blast. I won't stay here another day. Clive and David, very fortunately, are not in the place, an' I'm goin' away this very day."

"But where can we go?" asked Frank.

"Go? Why, to Verony."

" But we've sent messages off to Verona."

" Messages ! " exclaimed Uncle Moses. " Pooh ! I don't believe they've done the first thing. An' mind you, they won't do anything till you pay 'em. You forgot to do that, Frank."

" So I did," said Frank. " 'Pon my word, I do believe they've done nothing."

" Of course," said Uncle Moses. " An' now we've got either to pay them, or go ourselves. Now, I've made up my mind that we've got to go ourselves. Don't say a word. Don't oppose me. It's no use. I'm bound to go. My mind's made up, and go I will this very day to Verony."

Mild as Uncle Moses usually was, Frank knew perfectly well that when he had once made up his mind to anything, he was utterly immovable. On the present occasion he forbore to make any objection. He saw also that it was perhaps the best thing to be done under the circumstances, and so both he and Bob acquiesced without a word in the new plan.

About two hours after this, Uncle Moses, with Frank and Bob, left Venice, and soon arrived at Verona.

CHAPTER XV.

*New Wanderings and more Stories. — The Espousals of
the Adriatic. — The Capture of Constantinople.*

IT was certainly a singular position in which our
young friends were thrown. Here were two
parties separated from one another, and yet
in the same city, in one another's vicinity, passing
and repassing over the selfsame track, without
either being aware of the neighborhood of the
other. Such a thing might be barely possible in
other cities, but in Venice it was the most natural
thing in the world.

On this day they came more closely than ever
upon one another's tracks. Bob had been arrested
early in the morning. Then came Vernon to the
police station with inquiries about Miss Lee.

Scarcely had he left, when Uncle Moses and
Frank came. Thus the two parties had been
brought into very close proximity. Yet Uncle
Moses and Frank, of course, had no idea of the
facts of the case, and Clive and David were in
equal ignorance.

When Vernon came back from the Police Bureau,
he was eagerly interrogated by Gracie. When he

told her that nothing had been heard, she looked disturbed.

" I'm beginning to be awfully anxious," said she. " I feel as though I ought to be doing something, and yet I cannot imagine what I can do. I'm afraid that something may have happened to poor dear auntie. She is so inexperienced in travel, and she grows so confused when anything goes wrong ! "

Vernon tried to reassure her.

" O, really, now," said he, " you must try and not give way to anxiety. It's natural, of course, for you to feel so; but you must remember that we are doing the very best we can. The police can do infinitely more than we ; they have their connections all through Italy ; they can telegraph and communicate in other ways with all possible places ; and they are sure of finding her. Besides, it is very probable that your aunt will seek their assistance at once."

" O, I'm sure she never will; the very mention of the police is terrible to her. She is very timid. And that's the worst of it. She has a horror of all the continental police, and would die rather than seek their assistance."

" Well," said Vernon, " if you feel that something more ought to be done, I will do it. If the police do not bring any definite information, I'll take a run to Verona myself, and that is the hardest thing in the world for me to do just now."

"O, I'm sure," said Gracie, "I don't want you to put yourself to trouble for my sake, or to leave Venice — or to — "

"Trouble!" said Vernon. "It isn't that; but you know — I, in fact — I don't like to — to leave you — even for a day — and if — that is, if your aunt were only safe, I should like to wait at least until we had seen the whole of Venice. And, at any rate, we can wait this one day. You do not want me to go away to-day — do you? You will give me one more day — won't you?"

Vernon spoke in a tone of entreaty that seemed to indicate very strong emotion. As for Gracie, she herself seemed somewhat agitated. She stole a hasty look at the eloquent face of the handsome young artist; then her eyes fell, and she murmured in a low voice, —

"O, no. I should be sorry — not to have another day — in Venice. I only meant that — that I felt guilty in enjoying myself — so much — you know —while poor auntie was perhaps in great misery about me. That's all."

At these words Vernon's face grew radiant.

"O, thank you — thank you," said he. "Then we shall have one more day of enjoyment, and you'll come with me to-day, and we'll see as much as possible, and then this evening I shall go to hear what the police have found out. After that we may arrange other plans."

This seemed quite agreeable to Gracie. The

assurances of Vernon seemed to quell her anxiety, and she gave herself up for that day to the enjoyment that might be had.

At the usual time the boat was ready, and first of all they went to the Arsenal.

This place, once the centre and the source of the naval power of Venice, was now all still and silent. The thousands of workmen, the hundreds of galleys, the noise, the tumult, the clouds of black smoke from boiling pitch and glowing furnaces, which once made the Arsenal of Venice one of the wonders of the world — all these things had passed away. The multitude of busy, artisans had dwindled to a few loiterers; the fleet had given place to three or four small barks; the noise and tumult of vast enterprises had been succeeded by languor and quiet.

Entering through the massive gateway, they walked around and surveyed the docks and warehouses. There was but little to gratify curiosity. The interest of the place lay in the past. After making the tour of the works, they seated themselves upon a bench, from which they had a view of the harbor, and gave themselves up to pleasant conversation.

"Isn't there any chance," asked David, "that Venice will again become a great naval station? I should think that now, being connected with Italy, and free, she might be made use of, and this Arsenal might become busier than ever."

"O, no," said Vernon; "there's no chance of that. Modern warfare requires a different place. The enormous iron-clads of Italy cannot come here. The galleys of old times required but little water. No vessels can come here but those of light draught. Venice cannot be even the Queen of the Adriatic. Trieste now has that position. By the by, have you ever heard of the espousals of the Adriatic?"

"I've heard of that ceremony," said Gracie; "but I should like to know more about it. Haven't you something in your manuscript that you can read?"

At this invitation, Vernon took his manuscript, and read from it

THE ESPOUSALS OF THE ADRIATIC.

Well, you know, Frederic Barbarossa, Roman Emperor, had been engaged in a long struggle with Pope Alexander. It was one of the greatest conflicts on record, and the two combatants fought with very different weapons. For the emperor had all the warriors of Germany at his back, and half of Italy; while the pope was armed with the terrors of superstition and the thunders of the church. Besides this, the pope was sustained by the valiant Lombard republics, who defied the utmost power of the emperor, and had resolved to perish from off the face of the earth rather than yield. The struggle was terrible. It raged through Germany and

Italy, but especially Italy; and at length the pope became an exile and a wanderer, flying from place to place. In the course of these wanderings he came to Venice.

There was some danger in receiving the illustrious fugitive, for Venice would thus encounter the wrath of the mighty emperor, who was as powerful on sea as on land. But the Venetians did not stop to count the cost. They received Pope Alexander with boundless respect and hospitality; and when the emperor sent a demand for the surrender of the pope, with a denunciation of war in case of refusal, the Venetians sent a haughty reply, and prepared for war.

The maritime power of the emperor was vast. He had on his side the united navies of Genoa, Pisa, and Ancona, which now, at his command, moved upon Venice, in order to attack the city, punish the insolent Venetians, and capture his mortal enemy the pope. But the Venetians did not wait for the arrival of the imperial fleet. They themselves sailed out to act on the aggressive. On coming in sight of it, they found it superior in numbers, and provided with the most formidable equipments. It was under the command of the son of the great emperor, and was regarded as invincible. It had been sent to crush Venice forever, and all the maritime resources of Frederic had been put forth in order to insure success. But they had quite miscalculated the strength of Ven-

ice. The Venetians, whom they expected to be-
siege, came forth, and began a fierce attack. A
bloody struggle followed, which lasted for six or
eight hours, and terminated in a complete victory
for Venice. The imperial fleet was destroyed. Its
vessels and sailors were all sunk or captured, and
among the prisoners was the emperor's son Otho.
Venice was saved: the pope was saved: and in
that victory began the downfall of Frederic.

The fleet came back with its long train of captured vessels, all gay with flags and streamers.
Venice sent forth all its population to swell the
triumphant procession, and first among those who
went to greet the victors was the pope. No one
knew so well as he the full meaning of this great
victory.

Alexander addressed the victorious doge with
words full of joyful congratulation. Then he presented him with a gold ring.

"Take this ring," said Alexander, "and with it
take, on my authority, the sea, as your subject.
Every year, on the return of this auspicious day,
you and your successors shall proclaim to posterity
that the right of conquest has subjugated the Adriatic to Venice as a spouse to her husband."

The doge took the ring, and the Venetians accepted the gift of the sea. Thenceforth for ages
they commemorated this great event by a solemn
ceremony. On every anniversary of this day the
doge, with all the chief nobility, went to hear mass

at the Cathedral of St. Mark. Then they proceeded to embark in the galley which had carried the doge to his triumph over the imperial fleet. Blazing with gold, and adorned with most costly ornaments and richest trappings, this galley, — the Bucentaur, —followed by innumerable smaller craft, proceeded through the canals to the mouth of the harbor. There the doge dropped the ring into the sea, with these words : —

" We wed thee with this ring, in token of our perpetual sovereignty."

The ceremony was always kept up, and was always associated with the proudest recollections of Venice. Hundreds of years passed away, but the old Bucentaur lived on. Repairs were constantly made, until, like the ship Argo, there remained not one of her original timbers ; yet still she was the Bucentaur, and as the Bucentaur she was used for this solemn ceremony until the Austrians came.

" As I said before," said Vernon, after a while, "the day of Venice is over forever. She can never again be a great naval station, although she may live on, and have some moderate amount of traffic. Formerly it was different. The ancient galleys were slightly constructed, and drew but little water. The fleets of Venice, with which she won her great triumphs, and with some of which the destinies of the world were decided, were also composed of galleys of shallow draught."

14

"Which was the greatest of all the exploits of Venice?" asked Gracie.

"Well," said Vernon, "there are two; and the question lies between them. One was the capture of Constantinople, the other was the battle of Lepanto. In both of these Venice had allies. But it seems to me that the capture of Constantinople was more glorious for her, for the reason that she took the lead in that great exploit, and her doge, old Dandolo, was the hero of the war. It was different with Lepanto. If you like, I will read about the capture of Constantinople."

Receiving the usual eager assent, Vernon went on to read

The Capture of Constantinople.

Venice had always been very closely connected with Constantinople. At first it was part of the Roman empire, and reverenced the emperor at Constantinople as supreme lord. Afterwards, as the city grew more powerful, the connection was but slight; yet still the Venetians looked upon the emperors of the East as the true Roman emperors, and considered those Germans who arrogated the title as barbarian pretenders. Commercial intercourse was constant and well sustained, and down to the time of the crusades the attitude of Venice towards the Eastern empire was, with a few exceptions, one of respectful friendship, together with an acknowledgment of the supreme rank of the the Roman emperor who ruled in Constantinople.

But with the crusades came other feelings. These great movements caused an immense increase in the power and resources of Venice. Her ships were needed to convey crusaders to the East, and to supply them while there with provisions and munitions of war. Her navies were needed to co-operate with the soldiers of the cross against the common enemy. With her growing power, Venice became more ambitious, and, in her eager desire to extend her commerce, she grew to look on Constantinople as an obstacle in her way. At the same time the Eastern empire, with its ruler and its capital, had incurred the wrath of the Western warriors. Those who returned brought back endless tales of the treachery of the Eastern Christians, and all Europe came to regard them as heretics, whose Christian faith was but a name, and who preferred plotting in the closet to fighting in the field. Time went on, and these feelings grew stronger. The church of the West and the church of the East parted asunder forever, with mutual curses. The Western Christians grew utterly estranged from their Eastern brethren, and various wrongs which Venetians had to undergo at Constantinople conspired with these other circumstances to make Venice foremost in hostility to the Eastern capital; and the policy of her rulers became such as made them always on the lookout for the opportunity to inflict some harm upon the hated city.

Under these circumstances a new crusade was

preached, and the warriors of the cross decided to go by water to their destination rather than undertake the perils of a land journey. Of all these perils none were more dreaded than the passage across the Dardanelles, for there they would be dependent upon the aid of the Eastern emperor; and all the West now looked upon him as a secret enemy, more to be feared than the sultan of the Turks himself. Venice, therefore, became the rendezvous for the crusaders, who gathered there in large numbers, while the leaders sought to make a bargain with the government for ships and supplies. The bargain was made, and the Venetians prepared a fleet for the expedition.

When the time came for payment, however, it was found that the crusaders could not raise the money; and although the chiefs of the expedition made the utmost personal sacrifices, and contributed all that they possessed and all they could borrow, still there remained a deficit of more than one third the required sum. The Venetians now came forward with a proposal. One of their colonies, named Zara, had recently revolted. It lay in the way of the expedition, and the doge offered to set forth at once if the crusaders would lend their assistance towards capturing Zara. This proposal was accepted, and the expedition set sail.

It was a gallant sight. The whole fleet consisted of five hundred vessels of all sizes; two hundred and fifty of these carried the troops, while seventy were laden with military engines for siege operations. Such a force as this proved irresistible to the people of Zara. The town was captured, and the crusaders began to turn their thoughts towards the Holy Land.

But now, while waiting here at Zara, an event occurred which once more diverted the crusade from its proper destination, and led to a result never dreamed of by its original projectors.

Some years before, the Emperor of Constantinople, Isaac Angelus, had been deposed and blinded by his brother Alexius. The son of the fallen emperor, who was also named Alexius, was imprisoned for some time, but at length managed to escape, and fled to Italy. His brother-in-law was Philip, the Roman emperor, and his intention was to seek a home at his court in Germany. On his way there he was astonished at the great throngs who were hastening towards Venice, and by the advice of his friends he sent a message to the crusaders, imploring their assistance towards the deliverance of his father, and the recovery of the crown of the Eastern empire. In reply, they sent messengers, with the young Prince Alexius, to the Emperor Philip, stating that if he would assist the crusaders towards the recovery of the Holy Land, they would help the prince towards the recovery of Constantinople.

Philip, in reply, said that he was unable to do anything; but Prince Alexius made promises of the

most attractive character, in order to gain their
assistance. He offered to put an end to the dis-
union between the Greek and Latin churches, to
bring the whole Eastern empire into submission to
the pope, to assist them with a large army towards
the conquest of Jerusalem, and added to this boundless offers of rewards in money, and honors, and
territory. But before he could accomplish this, it
would be necessary for the crusaders to put him
and his father in power, and thus the siege of Constantinople would have to precede the crusade in
the Holy Land.

There were vehement debates over this proposal; but at length it was accepted, and the expedition set sail for Constantinople, and the Prince
Alexius, who had joined the crusaders at Zara,
went with them. Their voyage was slow and de-
liberate. They stopped at several places, where
they were peaceably received, and at length came
within sight of the great capital of the East. The
historian of the expedition tells the feelings of
the crusaders at the magnificent sight that burst
upon them. "When they contemplated," said he,
"the walls and goodly towers that enclosed it
around, the gay palaces and glittering churches
that seemed innumerable, the immense dimensions
of the city, denoting that it was the Queen of the
Earth, they could hardly believe their senses; nor
was there any man, however bold, whose heart did
not tremble within him. This was no marvel, for

never since the creation of the world had such an
enterprise been attempted by such a handful of
men."

But the Eastern empire had fallen upon evil
days. A few years before, when the Emperor
Manuel was reigning, such an expedition as this
would have been beaten back on its first appearance, and pursued to wreck and ruin. For in those
days the dock-yards of Constantinople could turn
out sixteen hundred ships of war, and the Greeks
were rulers of all the Eastern waters. But the
present emperor was attentive to nothing except
pleasure and personal indulgence; the care of affairs was handed over to corrupt officials; the fleet
had gone to decay; the army was almost extinct;
and even though ample notice had been given of
the approach of the crusaders, still such was the
general mismanagement, that no preparations had
been made to oppose them, and the capital of the
East lay exposed to their attack, itself almost defenceless. The only defence against the hostile
fleet was a stout chain, which had been stretched
across the harbor, behind which were twenty galleys, all that remained of the mighty navy of the
Eastern empire. To such an extreme of weakness
had the capital been reduced by the misgovern-
ment of Alexius.

Ten days were taken up in preparations, after
which the fleet of the crusaders bore down upon
the chain. For a time it withstood the assault; but

at last, one vessel of immense size, bearing down
with all its force, succeeded in breaking the cable.
The whole crusading navy followed, and the twenty
galleys inside were all destroyed or captured.

Having thus forced their way into the harbor,
they waited a few days longer in order to decide
about the best mode of attack. It was at length
resolved to make a combined assault by sea and
land, the Venetian warriors fighting from their galleys, and the crusaders on the land. The preparations for the attack were very extensive, and many
days were taken up in landing the troops, in preparing the engines, and in making the galleys
ready for an assault from the sea side. The preparations of the crusaders were rather simple, for
they trusted more to personal valor than to military
machines; but the Venetians, who trusted to both,
made far more elaborate arrangements. The galleys were filled with warlike engines, adapted to
hurl every variety of missile weapons into the city.
They were covered with raw hides, so as to be
protected from the terrible Greek fire; and they
had suspended rope-ladders from their yard-arms,
by means of which they could let themselves down
upon the walls. These yards, with their rope-
ladders, acted like draw-bridges, and let down
the Venetians upon the heads of the astonished
Greeks.

Their galleys, arranged in a single line, which
extended for nearly the whole length of the city

wall, sailed in close, discharging clouds of arrows, and stones, and other missiles. The galleys came up close to the walls, where the Greeks fought with much spirit, and poured torrents of Greek fire upon them. But the precautions taken were successful, and not much harm was done in this way. The yards were lowered, and the Venetians sought to descend. For a long time, however, they were slain as they came near the wall, until it seemed impossible to obtain a footing, and the Venetians, discouraged, began to relax their efforts.

And now it was that one hero came forward, and by a single act of valor changed the fortune of the day, and won for himself immortal glory. This hero was not an ardent youth, with all his future before him, eager to win name and fame by one bold stroke. It was the highest citizen of Venice, one who had distinguished himself by a long life of noble deeds, and might now have chosen to rest on his laurels. But though over eighty years of age, and blind also, the enthusiastic valor of the Doge Dandolo, which had impelled him to lead this expedition, now raised him to the foremost place of danger and of honor. Standing upon the prow of his galley, he had learned the progress of the fight; and now, when his forces were wavering, he ordered his men to run the galley ashore. Then, holding the banner of St. Mark, he leaped out, and was first upon the land. His men rushed after him to sustain him. The other galleys, who had seen this, did the same, and the whole host of Venetian warriors, impelled by the example of the doge, rushed anew to the assault, this time with such fury that the Greeks were driven out, and the whole line of sea-wall, with twenty-five towers, was seized and occupied.

The crusaders had fared differently. The attack which they made on the land side had been repelled, and the Greeks in vast numbers rushed out to take the offensive. The crusaders were compelled to take refuge behind their intrenchments, and in this position they sent to Dandolo, begging for assistance. In this emergency, if the emperor had been animated by any manly spirit, he could have overwhelmed the crusading host; but the same weakness that had made the capital defenceless against the hostile fleet, now made him falter before a determined foe. He sounded a retreat, and led his forces back to the city.

Yet still the peril of the crusaders was great; and the Venetians, though they held the wall, had to look forward to fierce attacks from superior numbers. "But behold," says the chronicler of this expedition, "the miracle of the Lord!" During the night an event took place which decided the contest. This was the flight of the cowardly emperor, who, hastily collecting what treasure he could, had embarked with his family on board a swift galley, and fled. No sooner had this become known, than the friends of the deposed emperor,

Isaac Angelus, went to restore him to his throne. He was awakened at midnight, and in these messengers the blind old man probably suspected at first the officers who were sent to take him to an ignominious death. But they came to bring him to life and honor; and after eight long years of miserable captivity, he was again clothed in the imperial robes, led by the hand to the palace, seated upon his former throne, and once more saluted as Roman emperor.

"This sounds like a very good ending to my story; but unfortunately it was only the beginning of the end. For the miseries of the aged Isaac in captivity were as nothing compared with those that yet lay before him. The wild promises of his son, the Prince Alexius, could never be fulfilled. Their very mention excited fearful commotion among the Greeks; their non-fulfilment roused the crusaders to rage and vengeance; then arose rebellions; the Prince Alexius was murdered; the Emperor Isaac died of a broken heart; the crusaders flung themselves once more upon the city. Once more they were successful. Constantinople was taken and given up to pillage and to flame, and the Eastern Roman empire was divided among the conquerors.

"And so my story ends."

CHAPTER XVI.

*Up the Grand Canal. — The Rialto. — The old original Bal-
lad of Shylock. — The Conspiracy of Thiepolo.*

LEAVING the Arsenal, they proceeded up the
Grand Canal, and at length came to that
great bridge, the most celebrated in existence, known as the Bridge of the Rialto. They
landed here and walked across it. It is one hundred and eighty-seven feet in length, and nearly
fifty in width, while on each side are small shops.
It crosses the canal by a single arch, which was once
regarded as one of the wonders of the world. But
the span of this bridge has since then been surpassed, and in vastness also the Rialto Bridge has
been left far behind by the gigantic structures of
the age of railroads.

In some things, however, the Rialto Bridge can
never be surpassed. In the first place, its beauty
must always be pre-eminent; then, again, its situation is unique; and not till another Venice arises out
of the sea can another bridge be made which shall
rival this. But above all, there is the charm of old
associations which throws around this bridge un-
ending glory. Around this as a common centre

revolves all the history of Venice: it is also the centre of a thousand legends; above all, it has received immortality from Shakespeare's mighty hand. Here before the mind many a form arises, and chief among them must ever be the Merchant of Venice, with his friends and his relentless enemy, Shylock.

Shylock. — What news on the Rialto? Who is he comes here?

Bassanio. — This is Signor Antonio.

With the very sight of the Rialto, these words come to the mind, and with these words there arises before the mind the whole of that wondrous and varied story.

It was of this that Vernon and his companions had most to say: and Vernon, who was an ardent admirer of Shakespeare, had a hundred things to tell them which threw fresh light on the familiar play. Among other things, he spoke of an old ballad, which must have been familiar to Shakespeare, and supplied him with some of the incidents of the play. He had it copied out in his manuscript, and it bore a quaint title.

"A new song showing the crueltie of Gernutus, a Jew, who, lending to a Marchant a hundred Crownes, would have a pound of his Flesh, because he could not pay him at the day appoynted. To the tune of Black and Yellow."

The First Part.

In Venice town, not long ago,
  A cruel Jew did dwell,
Who lived all on Usurie,
  As Italian writers tell.

Gernutus called was the Jew
  Which never thought to die,
Nor never yet did any good
  To them in streets that lie.

His life was like a Barrow Hog
  That liveth many a day,
Yet never once doth any good
  Until men will him slay;

Or like a filthy heap of dung
  That lieth in a hoard,
Which never can do any good
  Till it be spread abroad.

So fares it with the Usurer;
  He cannot sleep in rest,
For fear the thief will him pursue
  To pluck him from his nest.

His heart doth think on many a wile
  How to deceive the poor;
His mouth is always full of muck,
  Yet still he gapes for more.

His wife must lend a shilling
  For every week a penny,
Yet bring a pledge that's double worth,
  If that you will have any.

And see likewise you keep your day,
  Or else you lose it all;
This was the living of the wife;
  Her cow she did it call.

Within that city dwelt that time
  A merchant of great fame,
Which, being distressed in his need,
  Unto Gernutus came,

Desiring him to stand his friend
  For twelvemonth and a day,
To lend to him a hundred crowns,
  And he for it would pay

Whatsoever he would demand of him,
  And pledges he should have.
" No," quoth the Jew, with fleering looks —
  " Sir, ask what you will have.

" No penny for the loan of it
  For one year you shall pay;
You may do me as good a turn
  Before my dying day:

" But we will have a merry jest
  For to be talked long;
You shall make me a bond, quoth he,
  That shall be large and strong.

" And this shall be the forfeiture :
  Of your own flesh a pound;
If you agree, make you the bond,
  And here is a hundred crowns."

" With right good will," the merchant said;
  And so the bond was made,
When twelve months and a day drew on
  That back it should be paid.

The merchant's ships were all at sea,
    And money came not in;
Which way to take, or what to do,
    To think he doth begin.

And to Gernutus straight he comes
    With cap and bended knee,
And said to him, " Of courtesy,
    I pray you bear with me."

" With all my heart," Gernutus said;
    " Command it to your mind;
In things of bigger weight than this
    You shall me ready find."

He goes his way; the day once past
    Gernutus doth not slack
To get a sergeant presently
    And clapped him on the back;

And laid him into prison strong,
    And sued his bond withal,
And when the judgment day was come
    For judgment he did call.

The merchant's friends came thither fast
    With many a weeping eye,
For other means he could not find,
    But he that day must die.

*" The second part of the Jewe's crueltie, setting
forth the mercifulnesse of the Judge towardes the
Marchant. To the tune of Blacke and Yellow."*

Some offered for his hundred crowns
    Five hundred for to pay,
And some a thousand, two, or three,
    Yet still he did deny.

And at the last ten thousand crowns
   They offered, him to save;
Gernutus said, " I will not gold,
   My forfeit I will have.

"A pound of flesh is my desire,
   And that shall be my hire."
Then said the judge, " Yet, good my friend,
   Let me of you desire

" To take the flesh from such a place
   As yet you let him live;
Do so, and lo an hundred crowns
   To thee here will I give."

" No, no," quoth he, " no judgment here,
   For this it shall be tried;
For I will have my pound of flesh
   From under his right side."

It grieved all the company
   His cruelty to see,
For neither friend nor foe could help
   But he must spoiled be.

The bloody Jew now ready is
   With whetted blade in hand,
To spill the blood of innocent
   By forfeit of his bond.

And as he was about to strike
   In him the deadly blow,
" Stay," quoth the judge, " thy cruelty, —
   I charge thee to do so.

" Since needs thou wilt thy forfeit have,
   Which is of flesh a pound,
See that thou shed no drop of blood,
   Nor yet the man confound.

15

" For if thou do, like murderer
  Thou here shalt hanged be;
Likewise of flesh, see that thou cut
  No more than 'longs to thee;

" For if thou take either more or less,
  To the value of a mite,
Thou shalt be hanged presently,
  As is both law and right."

Gernutus now wax'd frantic mad,
  And wot not what to say.
Quoth he at last, " Ten thousand crowns
  I will that he shall pay.

" And so I grant to set him free."
  The judge doth answer make,
" You shall not have a penny given, —
  Your forfeiture now take."

And at the last he doth demand
  But for to have his own.
" No," quoth the judge, " do as you list,
  Thy judgment shall be shown.

" Either take your pound of flesh," quoth he,
  " Or cancel me your bond."
" O, cruel judge," then quoth the Jew,
  " That doth against me stand."

And so with griping, grievèd mind,
  He biddeth them farewell,
And all the people praised the Lord
  That ever this heard tell.

Good people that do hear this song,
  For truth I dare well say,
That many a wretch as ill as he
  Doth live now at this day,

That seeketh nothing but the spoil
  Of many a wealthy man,
And for to trap the innocent
  Deviseth what they can.

From whom the Lord deliver me,
  And many a Christian, too,
And send to them like sentence eke
  That meaneth so to do.

"What do you think of the old ballad?" asked Vernon, as he ended.

"I think," said Gracie, in a candid tone, "that it is sad doggerel."

"Yes," said Vernon, "so it is; but then it is interesting, after all, for it shows how Shakespeare made up his play."

"I thought," said Clive, "that he invented it all."

"No," said Vernon; "he never made up any of his plays in that way. He always took some story such as this, and in that way made his play. He showed his inventive power in transforming a dull and prosaic narrative to a play where all the characters are endowed with life and action, so that they live in our memories always, and we cannot help thinking of them as though they were real persons. To most people Shylock is as real a character as Carlo Zeno, or Faliero, or old Dandolo."

"I should think so," said Gracie; "for how many people do you suppose know anything about those others?"

"Well, then," said Vernon, "as real as Alexander the Great, or Julius Cæsar, or Napoleon Bonaparte."

"But in the ballad," said David, "no mention is made of Portia or the caskets."

"No," said Vernon; "that was all taken from another story."

"Another story? Why couldn't Shakespeare have invented that?"

"Certainly he could," said Vernon; "but he didn't. He took these stories, and used them as foundations. That doesn't make his plays any the worse — does it?"

"Well, no, I suppose not," said David; "but it seems as though it takes something away from his genius."

"Not at all," said Vernon. "If it wasn't for Shakespeare, no one would attach any importance to these tales and ballads. No one else had his power. He stood alone — a mighty magician; and, as Dryden says, —

'Within that circle none durst walk but he.'

As to the story of the caskets, that is found in a collection of tales, very popular in old times, called the Gesta Romanorum."

"I remember," said Clive. "I have the book, translated, of course. The stories are full of all sorts of marvels. They're not to be compared to the Arabian Nights."

"O, no," said Vernon; "of course not. Few people can take any interest now in the Gesta Romanorum; but the Arabian Nights are as popular with us as they ever were with the Arabians themselves, and are far better known in London, Paris, and New York, than they are in Cairo, Constantinople, or Teheran."

"I have something else in my manuscript," said Vernon, after a pause, "that is connected with the Rialto, and if you like I will read it. It is about a famous conspiracy, which had very important results."

"Read it, by all means," said Gracie.

So Vernon went on to read

THE CONSPIRACY OF THIEPOLO.

Venice was often threatened by dangers from without; but in the year 1310 a danger arose from within which produced greater effects than all of the others. These effects consisted in a complete change in the constitution, and the adoption of a new order of things, by which the old popular freedom perished utterly, and the once free republic became cursed with a tyranny which ultimately became a dark Reign of Terror, and by its prolonged duration and awful power made the very name of the state synonymous with all that is most detestable to human nature. Other revolutions have taken place in proud republics, by which their liberties have been subverted; but never has there been any change so miserable as that by which Venice passed from its ancient government to the mysterious and terrible domination of the Council of Ten.

The rule of the Doge Gradenigo had been marked by misfortunes of no common kind; and to crown all, a quarrel with the pope had resulted in an interdict which weighed heavily on all classes of the people. The nobles had certainly less cause for discontent than any others; but on this occasion it was from this very class that the movement arose which aimed at nothing less than the overthrow of the government and a complete revolution in the state.

It was set on foot by one Thiepolo, a noble, who belonged to one of the chief families, and among whose ancestors had been several doges. His own aim was one of ambition. He thought the ducal dignity his own due, and succeeded in associating with himself several other nobles, who hoped in this way to further their own ambitious designs. The movement spread rapidly. It was ably planned; the secret, though involving so many, was carefully kept; and so widely extended were the connections of this conspiracy, that arrangements were made for assistance from Padua. The insurgents in the city, who themselves were very numerous, were to be aided by a large force from the latter place, and the 16th of June was fixed upon as the day for the rising.

But though the movement had not been betrayed, it had, nevertheless, been noticed and suspected. The keen eyes of the doge had marked the gatherings and other movements of bands of men who seemed bent upon some unusual purpose. This he communicated to the Council, who at once took the alarm, and proceeded in all haste to guard against the danger that threatened. Armed men were, therefore, stationed at various points, especially at the Arsenal and at the Piazza of St. Mark; and on the very night before the rising all these precautionary measures were completed.

The appointed morning came. It was stormy. The rain poured down in torrents, and the wind blew a gale. All this was regarded by the insurgents as favorable. The arrangements had all been made, and various bands had received instructions to seize different posts in the city. The place which was to be assailed by Thiepolo was the Rialto. His part was accomplished with complete success. There was no resistance. The bridge was taken and occupied, and the surrounding districts were strongly fortified.

Far different, however, was the fate of the others. The chief attack, after that of Thiepolo, was made upon the Piazza of St. Mark. But no sooner had they reached the place than, to their amazement, they found it occupied by superior forces. A fierce fight ensued. The insurgents, instead of fighting for victory, were compelled to fight for liberty and life. The thought that they had been betrayed utterly demoralized them. Those who were able to fly did so at once, and the rest, after a brief struggle, were captured.

From these fugitives Thiepolo learned the news, and at once perceived that all was lost. He only sought now for his own safety. Seizing a boat, he set out for the main land, and succeeded in effecting his escape, while his followers, now deprived of a leader, dispersed in all directions.

Such was the conspiracy of Thiepolo — an event which, in itself, would be but of slight importance among the immense movements of Venetian history, but which, from its important consequences, must be considered as holding a foremost place among them.

The feeling of the government seems to have been one of utter consternation. All felt the necessity of guarding against the possibility of another attempt like this. Rome, in one of her periods of trouble, appointed a supreme ruler called a Dictator. Venice now did the same, with the important difference that instead of one dictator there were ten. Absolute power was given to them for punishing the rebels, and for devising means of guarding against a repetition of such a plot. The new Council was invested with perfect sovereignty over all in the state, and freedom from all responsibility. At first they were appointed for ten days. This period was then extended six times; then it was prolonged to a year; then to five years; then to ten; and finally it was made permanent. For from the very first the Council of Ten had begun to rule by mystery and terror; and so effective was the machinery which they organized, that they at length placed their power on an immovable basis.

CHAPTER XVII.

*The outer Sea. — A distant View of Venice. — The Brides
of Venice. — The Story of the War of Chiozza.*

WHILE Vernon had been reading these stories, the gondola had been moving along the Grand Canal, and by the time that he had finished, it had come out into the open sea. They looked out and saw a wide extent of water, with here and there an island, upon which were houses and churches. These islands lay separated from Venice, and were inhabited chiefly by the lower orders. They formed what may be called the suburbs of Venice.

The boat passed along the outskirts of the city, at some distance, from which they could see to the best advantage the wonderful appearance of Venice as it lay before them, with the waters encompassing it on every side, rising out of the sea abruptly — a marvellous, an unequalled spectacle.

" I am thinking," said Gracie, after a long pause of silent admiration, " of some poetry which is far prettier than your old ballad."

" What is it ? " asked Vernon, eagerly. " Say it."

" O, it's familiar enough to all of you. It's Byron's verses."

"Say it, at any rate," said Vernon. "I should love to hear you."

Gracie threw a pretty little look at him, half embarrassment and half consent, after which she recited some verses : —

"I stood in Venice, on the Bridge of Sighs,
　A palace and a prison on each hand :
　I saw from out the waves her structures rise
　As from the stroke of an enchanter's wand.
　A thousand years their cloudy wings expand
　Around me, and a dying glory smiles
　O'er the far times, when many a subject land
　Looked to the Wingéd Lion's marble piles,
Where Venice sat in state, throned on her hundred isles.

"She looks a sea Cybele, fresh from ocean,
　Rising with her tiara of proud towers
　At airy distance with majestic motion,
　A ruler of the waters and their powers ;
　And such she was ; her daughters had their dowers
　From spoils of nations, and the exhaustless East
　Poured in her lap all gems in sparkling showers.
　In purple was she robed, and of her feast
Monarchs partook, and deemed their dignity increased."

Gracie said these verses with deep feeling and fine emphasis. Her voice was sweet and musical, and all listened in deep silence.

"I wish," said Vernon, "that you could go on and say the whole canto. I can only express my feelings by quoting Milton : —

'The angel ended, and in Adam's ear
　So charming left his voice, that he a while
　Thought him still speaking, still stood fixed to hear.'"

"Nonsense!" said Gracie, with a blush and a smile. "But, Mr. Vernon, haven't you something more to read?"

Vernon drew forth his manuscript, and said,—

"O, well, if you wish it."

"Wish it? Most certainly we do."

And so Vernon began to read the story of

THE BRIDES OF VENICE.

Once upon a time, he began, it was the fashion among the Venetian aristocracy to celebrate their marriages on the eve of the Festival of the Purification of the Virgin. Of course marriages took place on other occasions also: but this was the favorite time, and also the most fashionable, so that there were always a number of weddings to be celebrated at once. The ceremonies always took place at Olivolo, which lies at the extreme end of the city, towards the east.

It was one of the greatest days in the year. All the friends of the bridal pairs would assemble, arrayed in their festive attire, and a large crowd of gondolas had to be collected, so as to convey the party to the place and back. Decorated with gay streamers, the little fleet used to pass through the city to the sound of lively music, followed by great numbers of spectators in other boats; and in this way they approached their destination. To this place the friends of the bridal pairs also would bring their bridal presents, which, being very numerous and costly, represented in the aggregate a large sum of money. It was this great prize which led to a daring attempt on the part of some ruffians from Istria.

Hearing of this ceremony and of the presents, the idea occurred to them of making a bold attempt to seize the wedding gifts. It was carried out very craftily and successfully. Coming to Venice in their ships, they landed in disguise at Olivolo, and concealed themselves there until the time of the ceremony. No one suspected danger. No one had come provided with arms, nor were there any guards of any kind about.

The ceremony began and went on, when suddenly, in the midst of it, with a wild, fierce shout, the Istrian brigands burst into the midst of the assembly. In an instant they had seized all the jewels and bridal presents. But already another idea had occurred to the ruffians; and this was, to seize the brides also. They would be a prize of far more value than gems or gold. Belonging to the noblest families of Venice, they could command a ransom of untold wealth. It was for this that the brigands seized them, and bore them away shrieking and fainting from their despairing friends. They then rowed to their ship, boarded it, and fled across the sea.

But there was no time for despair. The bereaved friends hurried back to the city. The doge summoned the citizens to arms. In a short time the waters were covered with a fleet of fierce pursuers, hurrying on the track of the brigands. First in the pursuit was a ship manned by the bridegrooms, who, with hearts almost bursting with fury and despair, had seized the swiftest galley in port, had set out first, and were now driving her through the water.

Far away they could see the ship that held their precious treasures — their brides. Had the brigands known better the intricate channels that surround the city, they could have effected their purpose. But they had become bewildered in one of the canals, and their pursuers gained rapidly on them, and at length reached them.

In the first fury of the attack, love was forgotten, and there was no thought of anything but vengeance. The brigands resisted obstinately; but such was the frenzy of the bridegrooms, that their resistance proved unavailing; and the whole band were slaughtered and thrown into the sea. When the rest of the Venetian fleet came up, all was over, and nothing now remained but to lead back the brides in triumph. They all returned to Olivolo. The ceremony was continued from the point at which it had been broken off, and the rescued brides were at last united to those whom they thought they had lost forever.

Venice is a great place for keeping alive the memories of past events; and among its various festivals the commemoration of the rescue of the brides always held a high place. Every year afterwards, on the anniversary of this day, various games and festivals took place, chief among which was a procession of Venetian ladies to the Church of Santa Maria Formosa, which is the church at Olivolo. Here also the doge came with another stately procession, and on landing, went through certain ceremonies which were designed to commemorate the events of that momentous day.

"I like early Venetian history," said Gracie, "ever so much better than later. It's not so dark or dreadful."

"It's more cheerful," said Vernon. "The state was free, and there was no Council of Ten, no spies, no secrecy, no horrors to make the blood run cold."

"At any rate," said David, "the history of Venice under the Council of Ten is more exciting. Don't you think so, Mr. Vernon? Think of the long list of harrowing tales that have made Venice famous. Shylock and Othello belong to the later period."

"Yes, and Otway's Venice Preserved," said Clive.

"And Schiller's Ghost Seer," said David.

"And some of Mrs. Radcliffe's, and Abellino, the Bravo of Venice."

Vernon laughed.

"O, go on, youngsters," said he. "When it comes to Abellino, I give up. I dare say you are better up in that work than I am."

"It seems to me," said Gracie, "that the Venetians were always rather politic and cautious than heroic. Is there anything in their history that shows them reduced to extremity like the Athenians with the Persian in their city? or like the Romans after Cannae? or like the Dutch at Leyden? or the French after Agincourt? I don't like people that are always cool and prudent. Now, if there is anything that shows us Venice in a more heroic mood, I should like to hear it."

"I think I can find something of that sort," said Vernon, turning over the leaves of his manuscript. "This will be different from anything that I have read thus far."

And with this he began to read

The War of Chiozza.

The year 1379 saw the darkest days in all the history of Venice, from her first beginning until her final fall. War had been raging with Genoa. The Lord of Padua, the bitterest enemy of Venice, was in league with the Genoese. The Venetian fleet under Admiral Pisani had been defeated at Pola. All the rest of her ships of war were far away, under the command of Carlo Zeno, and nothing was left in the city to maintain her honor upon the Adriatic. In the midst of all this, her enemies hastened to take advantage of her distress, and began a combined movement upon Venice, which they hoped would efface her from the list of nations.

When they heard of the approach of the enemy, the Venetians hastened to complete all possible measures for defence. All the principal channels that led to the city were blockaded by means of piles or sunken ships; the outposts were fortified and strengthened; most of all, they sought to strengthen the outlying post of Chiozza, which was the key to the harbor, and the possession of which would inevitably be the object of the first and fiercest struggle. Of the importance of this post the Genoese were as well aware as the Venetians; and therefore it was upon this that they made their first attack. The struggle that followed was a bloody one; the Genoese fighting for victory, the Venetians for self-preservation. But the defenders were far outnumbered; and at last Chiozza, upon which so much depended, was torn from their grasp, its defenders perished, and the news of this great calamity, when it was made known to the Venetian, seemed to tell them that all was lost.

A panic spread through the city. The people assembled in despairing crowds in the Grand Piazza, awaiting in silence the action of the government. The Grand Council in session were in no less despair. The usual calmness and fortitude which had distinguished the Venetian government now disappeared, and they could think of no other course of action than a humble petition for peace on any terms. An embassy was sent to the enemy, taking with them some Genoese prisoners of eminent rank, who were freed without ransom, and also a sheet of blank paper, which was to be filled up by the enemy with any conditions which they thought proper. The only proviso which the ambassadors were charged to make was, that Venice should remain independent.

On the reception of this embassy, the Lord of Padua would have been satisfied with this submission of Venice on his own terms, and would have been willing to concede the independence of the state: but the Genoese Admiral Doria, animated by all the jealous hate of his country, was determined upon a far deeper vengeance.

"Take back your captives," said he, alluding to the Genoese who had accompanied the embassy. "Ere many hours I shall deliver both them and all their comrades. By God above, ye signors of Venice, you must expect no peace either from the Lord of Padua, or from our republic, till we ourselves have bridled the horses of your St. Mark. Place but the reins once in our hands, and we shall know how to keep them quiet for the future."

This reply plunged the Venetians into deeper despair. The Council remained in session, the people gathered around, and nothing now appeared before them except a hopeless resistance, which could only terminate in the ruin of the state. In this dark hour the people thought of Pisani. This great man, the popular idol, had until recently been the chief admiral of the Venetian navy, but his defeat at Pola had led to his humiliation and imprisonment. The people could now think of no other so capable as he to rescue the state from its peril. Their doge was in despair, their Council was helpless. There was no one who could say what was yet to be done, or direct all that living mass of fiery valor, which, without a leader, was so helpless. And so there went forth a universal cry for Pisani, which could not be resisted. The Council and the doge were glad enough to yield, and sacrifice their dignity and their jealousy for the safety of the commonwealth. The prison doors were thrown open: Pisani came forth, and once more found himself the leader of the Venetians; but this time it was in the darkest hour of her despair, and he himself was the last hope of his country.

Pisani showed no resentment for his wrongs, but with self-sacrificing patriotism at once devoted himself to the work of rescuing the state from its danger. All Venice felt the influence of his genius. His spirit was visible everywhere. Every man was put to work. The approaches to the city were strengthened with fresh blockades, and larger defences. The mechanics were gathered into the dock-yards to construct new ships of war, or transform merchant vessels into galleys. Every able-bodied man was armed and drilled. In an astonishingly short space of time the results of

Pisani's genius and energy were perceptible. A fleet made its appearance, which grew larger every day. Manned with Venetian citizens, who were for the most part unacquainted with war, this fleet was incessantly kept at maritime exercises; and the Genoese, who kept the blockade, saw in astonishment a new fleet arising out of nothing, and performing evolutions under their own eyes.

All classes were pervaded by the heroic spirit of their leader. Never in the history of the world were there greater examples of patriotic devotion and self-sacrifice. The young men all took up arms. The women gave their jewels, and worked incessantly with their hands for their country. Old men, who could do nothing else, gave up their wealth. Entire fortunes were presented to the state, and vast debts were given up by creditors; plate, jewels, and treasure were heaped into the public coffers; even the priests and monks took up arms in the holy cause of their country. There was one tradesman who undertook the maintenance of a thousand men; another equipped a ship of war; while the poorer artisans associated together to maintain companies of soldiers. One of the most touching examples of this self-sacrifice was seen in the aged Matteo Fascolo. He had been a wealthy citizen of Chiozza, but had lost all by the capture of that place. He took his two sons and presented them to the magistrates. "If my estate," said he, " were such as it once was, I would give it all for the requirements of my country : but our lives are now all that are left to me and my sons. Dispose of us as you think best. Employ us either by land or sea, and let us rejoice in the thought that what little we still possess is devoted to our country."

At length, by means of such intense and prolonged exertions on the part of all classes of the state, Pisani found himself in possession of a force with which he might hope to compete with the enemy on equal terms. That enemy had already gone into winter quarters behind Chiozza, where the most of their ships were dismantled, and of the whole fleet only three galleys were in active service. Chiozza was built, like Venice, upon a group of islands, surrounded by sand-banks. The approaches to this place from the sea were by means of two channels, one of which was called Chiozza, and the other Broudolo. The plan which Pisani had conceived was, to make a combined attack upon these two channels, and block them up. In this case the Genoese fleet would be shut out altogether from the sea. They would then be blockaded in turn. At the same time the Venetian fleet, under Carlo Zeno, which was cruising abroad, might soon be expected home, in which case their enlarged forces would enable them to have the Genoese at their mercy.

On the 23d of December the Venetian armament set forth upon its bold attempt. Its departure was celebrated with solemn services at St. Mark's. The doge himself went with the fleet, and swore never to return unless victorious. The fleet consisted of fifty ships of war, sixty armed merchant vessels, three hundred boats filled with troops, and two large hulks filled with stone and rubbish.

They made their entrance first into the Strait of Chiozza, and landed five thousand men. The Genoese hurried forth to encounter them, and a battle ensued, in which the Venetians were driven back to their boats. This, however, was part of the design of Pisani, who brought on the battle for the purpose of engaging the attention of the Genoese, and distracting it from his chief purpose. While the battle was going on, the hulks were towed into the channel. The Genoese, in their three galleys, made a desperate assault upon the hulks, and in the course of the struggle they were sunk. The Venetian flotilla then advanced with huge masses of stone and ballast, which they heaped over the sunken ships. After this, strong rows of piles were driven in, and by the end of the following day this channel was completely blocked up; while the Venetian fleet effectually prevented the Genoese from trying to remove the obstructions.

The other channel of Brondolo still remained, and here the Venetians sailed as soon as possible. It was guarded by strong posts on the shore, and a fierce conflict took place between the Genoese and the Venetians, during which the latter succeeded in their purpose : for as they had now the superiority on the sea, they were able to block up this channel also.

The Genoese were now effectually shut in ; the only channels by which they could escape were closed up, and the obstructions were incessantly guarded by the Venetians. But the Genoese were not idle. They were well aware of the danger in which they were. Fierce fights took place incessantly as the Genoese strove to remove the obstructions and force the barriers; but in all of these the Venetians maintained the advantage. The struggle between the two now became most exhaustive ; on the part of the Genoese there were incessant attacks, on the part of the Venetians never-ending vigilance. For the Genoese there was nothing else to be done ; but the Venetians, who had already accomplished so much, had their own city behind them ; and the thought of this, the longing after home, and the severe labors of constant watching and continuous fighting, all tended to dampen their ardor. Murmurs arose. The men clamored for some rest or respite ; and at length the whole fleet became so mutinous that Pisani was compelled to yield. He therefore promised to return to Venice, but required a further service of forty-eight hours, in which time he hoped that the fleet of Carlo Zeno might arrive.

Never were forty-eight hours passed in greater suspense, and never did greater issues depend upon the events of that time. Like Columbus, when he had been forced to make a similar promise to his sailors, Pisani waited anxiously, looking out over the waters to detect some signs of that which was to determine so much. At the same time the Genoese looked forth over the same waters with equal anxiety, for they, too, expected aid and re-enforcements; and all their hopes depended upon relief from home.

At length, before the time had expired, sails were seen in the distance. Genoese and Venetian now watched with equal anxiety to see what that fleet might be. Pisani waited in a suspense as great as that with which Napoleon waited at Waterloo, to know whether the approaching force might be that of Grouchy or Blucher.

At last all suspense ended, and as the fleet approached, the Venetians rose up from doubt and dark terror to wild and enthusiastic joy. The fleet was theirs; it was the long-looked-for fleet of Carlo Zeno.

The struggle now went on more furiously than ever; the Venetians eager to bring the war to an end, the Genoese animated by love of life, the hope of escape, and every motive that is most powerful in the human heart. In the midst of the conflict, the great Doria perished; and though he thus escaped the calamities of the future, still the loss of their leader made that future darker than ever for the Genoese.

On the 19th of February a combined attack was made by land and sea upon the Genoese posts. In the course of the struggle, the Genoese made an attempt to get into the rear of Zeno's force; but a brilliant movement on the part of that commander led to their defeat. In the course of their flight a bridge broke down beneath the weight of the multitude upon it, and the fugitives, thus cut off, were all slaughtered helplessly.

After these terrible losses, the Genoese shut themselves up, and acted on the defensive, animated only by the hope of relief from home. At last a fleet appeared, which proved to be the one that had been so long desired. The Venetians had anticipated this; they had made all their preparations, and had decided upon their best policy. That policy was to maintain the blockade, which now not only shut in the besieged, but also kept the re-enforcements from reaching them. As the new fleet approached, the Venetians watched them in the security of an unassailable position: and the Genoese on both sides perceived in anguish of soul that no communication was possible between them. The Genoese Admiral Maruffo, who commanded the relieving fleet, reconnoitred every position, but found each in turn impassable; while the wretched garrison, who had watched his approach with such feverish joy, now beheld his retreat, and burst forth into passionate lamentations and cries of despair.

The garrison still held out. Provisions had long since failed them, and they were reduced to the last privations. But surrender to an implacable foe seemed worse than death; and they endured everything before consenting to that. On one occasion a desperate attempt was made to pass over to the main land by means of rafts and small boats; but in this they were unsuccessful. The Venetians pursued them in boats, and all perished.

At last all was over. The Genoese garrison had to make an unconditional surrender. The Venetians held victory within their grasp, and entered into the fortress that had so long repelled them. Out of that proud armament which had brought Venice down to the lowest depths of despair, they found but nineteen galleys left, and only a little over four thousand men, whose emaciated frames bore witness to their prolonged sufferings.

On the surrender of the garrison, the Genoese Admiral Maruffo retreated; and the Venetians returned in triumph to their city. At the head of his victorious host, the doge entered the city in the Bucentaur; and that day was the most glorious in all the annals of Venice.

CHAPTER XVIII.

Afloat. — In a Gondola. — Romantic Situation. — The Story of the three Artists.

THE gondola still glided along upon the outer waters.

"This is delightful," said Vernon. " I feel like singing, 'I'm afloat, I'm afloat.' Here we are gliding along, youth at the prow, and pleasure at the helm; youth in the persons of Clive and David, who are eagerly trying to make out places from the map of the city, while pleasure at the helm may be represented by our good selves, as we sit here in this snug little cabin, bent on enjoying ourselves."

" I wish," said Gracie, " that I could thank you sufficiently for the pleasure that you have given me, Mr. Vernon. There has been only one drawback — only one."

" Yes," said Vernon : " I know. But still let us hope that we shall hear something this evening about your aunt. If not, I will set to work myself. At the same time I hope to have good news this evening."

" I hope so, I'm sure," said Gracie.

" If I don't hear anything, I will go myself, much as I hate to break up these delightful interviews. I hope," continued he, in a low voice, " that I have made it pleasant for you."

" I'm sure," said Gracie, " you must have seen for yourself how pleasant it has been. I'm afraid I've been enjoying myself too much. I've forgotten my poor auntie."

" Well, perhaps I've forgotten to do my duty, too," said Vernon. " I've been thinking so much of you that I've forgotten your aunt.

> ' With thee conversing, I forget all time;
> But neither breath of morn, when she ascends,
> With charm of earliest birds, nor rising sun,
> Nor grateful evening mild, nor silent night,
> With this her solemn bird, nor walk by noon,
> Nor glittering starlight, without thee is sweet.' "

" That's from Milton," said Gracie, with a pretty little air of embarrassment. " You appear to take great delight in Paradise Lost, Mr. Vernon."

" Yes; but I take greater delight in a present Paradise," said Vernon, looking at her with deep meaning.

Gracie's eyes fell before his, and her embarrassment grew greater. Vernon drew nearer to her, and was just on the point of saying something more; but unfortunately at that moment Clive and David came in, arguing hotly about some point on which they wished to have his decision. The decision was promptly made, and in Clive's favor;

after which Vernon looked as if he thought that the boys might possibly want to go out again. But the boys had no idea of anything of the kind. On the contrary, they deposited themselves in easy attitudes on the soft cushions, and Clive said, —

" Would it be too much, Mr. Vernon, to ask you to read another of your stories ? "

" O, do," said Gracie. " Haven't you another story about artist life ? "

Vernon drew a long breath, and took up his manuscript with an air of resignation. His little remark to Gracie had thus to be postponed. What he read was the following : —

The Three Artists.

Sagredo, Pezaro, and Urso were three young artists who had studied under Titian. Of these, Sagredo had been the master's favorite. He was distinguished by his warmth of coloring, his fertility of conception, and his marvellous power of indicating by delicate touches the most subtile variations in the expression of the human countenance. Pezaro was an artist of superior abilities ; in drawing and coloring he was quite equal to the other ; he was also most painstaking, and never grudged any labor that might make his work better ; but then he lacked the rare power of conception which was evinced by Sagredo, and the equally rare power of putting those conceptions upon canvas. As a copyist, he was almost perfect ; but in an original picture he failed to exhibit that mastery over the world of passion and expression which was so prominent a feature in Sagredo's works. Urso, again, was different from both. Ardent and impetuous, he had vivid conceptions, but he had not the patience to work them out. He tried to grasp at perfection by a sudden rush, and could not wait to seek after it by slow and steady application. His works indicated great general effects, which might appeal to the common crowd, but not the finished creations of an artist who works for the cultivated classes. In fact, anything like careful finish was out of his power. He boasted of his rapidity, and sneered at the slow and laborious efforts of Sagredo, whom he always depreciated, and of whom, at the same time, he was bitterly jealous.

The annual Easter exhibition of paintings was approaching. It was to take place in the Museo Pamfili; and great was the excitement among all those who took an interest in art — a class which in Venice was a very large one. Many competitors had given in their names, but the chief interest rested upon Sagredo and Pezaro. Among the others was Urso. As he was in the habit of sneering at everything, so he directed his sneers at these exhibitions. He declared the judges to be partial and prejudiced. For his part, he said, he did not intend to kill himself for a lot of old women. He intended to enjoy himself, and dash off something at the latest moment. Genius, he asserted, disdains drudgery. A work of art ought to show something more than manual labor. His works showed brains, and if the judges had brains they would decide differently; but then they always decided by a set of formal rules, and had no soul to perceive the subtile beauty of a great and original work.

All this, and more of the same sort, was listened to approvingly by a little crowd of admirers who had gathered around Urso, who were impressed by his positiveness, by his constant depreciation of others, and by his vigorous self-assertion.

The appointed day at last came. All the pictures were hung, and curtains protected each one from the dust, and also served to conceal them until the moment should arrive when each should be revealed. A large crowd assembled, full of curiosity, and among them was the great master, Titian, who was always interested in the progress of his pupils.

Picture after picture was disclosed, and each received its proper comments. That of Pezaro was universally admired. It represented the Flight into Egypt — an old subject, which, however, was treated with much originality — a burning plain — a solitary palm tree — the holy family resting — the ass tethered near at hand, and cropping some scant herbage. Titian looked and smiled approvingly.

A few others were uncovered, and then came

Urso's picture. It was a great blaze of coloring, coarsely dashed on, and was a palpable appeal to the popular prejudice and self-conceit. The subject was the Genius of Venice — a nude figure, with a halo round the head, and a crown of stars was represented flying over the waves. In the sky above were Fame, Victory, Peace, Fortune, and twenty more allegorical figures; in the water beneath was Neptune with a great crowd of Tritons and Nereids; while upon a distant shore stood a row of other figures representing the states of Europe. Some were loud in applause; others were silent; Titian raised his brows, and then looked away.

Urso saw this somewhat contemptuous movement.

"It's not in the old man's style," he whispered to a friend; "he don't understand it at all. But his day is over. My turn will come, for I'm going to found a new school."

At last, Sagredo's picture was reached, and all waited, full of eager expectation.

The curtain was drawn.

For a moment all stood staring in perplexity, and then looked at one another in wonder. The picture — what did this mean? What was this that they saw before them? It was nothing! Nothing was there but a confused blur, that looked like a great daub from some coarse and hasty brush. Amazement seized upon all, and amazement was followed by confusion. Titian, who had awaited the drawing of the curtain with a smile of pleasant anticipation, looked around in astonishment. Pezaro stared at Sagredo, and all the rest did the same. For it seemed at first as though this enigma could be solved only by him; and there was a thought that in this apparent mockery there might be some hidden meaning.

But this notion was soon dispelled. They saw Sagredo, pale as death, standing with his eyes fixed on the blurred painting, with agony in his face. He stood thus for some time, staring and silent, and at length burst into tears.

"What is this?" he cried. "I never knew that I had an enemy."

At this the whole truth burst upon them. Sagredo had an enemy. He had been dealt with most foully. Who was he? Who could he be? How could he have done this? Such were the indignant questions which each one asked the other, and the murmurs that first arose deepened into indignant demands for an investigation into this.

The janitor was summoned and interrogated. But he could tell nothing. In vain they threatened him with the vengeance of the law. The threat only served to reduce the miserable man to the borders of idiocy. It was plain that he knew nothing about it. And so the mystery remained as dark as ever; and no one could conceive how or why this cruel deed had been done.

17

In the midst of this, Urso went up to Sagredo, and condoled with him.

"It's a fiendish act," said he, "a devilish act. To me, of course, it would not be much; but for you, who work so slowly, it must be hard. Why, it spoils the work for a whole year."

"Yes," said Sagredo, sadly, "a whole year's work is ruined — and more too."

"O, well," said Urso; "you should do as I do; work fast — don't be a drudge."

Sagredo shook his head wearily.

"Every one," said he, "must work in accordance with his own taste and temper."

It was, as Urso said, a fiendish act, but still the deed had been done, and there was no help for it. The judges, in awarding the prize, could only decide from the actual pictures before them, and could not, of course, take any notice of a blurred canvas. And so in their decision they awarded the prize to Pezaro.

No sooner was this announced than Pezaro burst forth.

"No," said he, indignantly, "I'll not take it. I saw Sagredo's picture. It was far — far — better than mine. Sagredo is far superior to me. I could be willing to be his pupil, except that I know that he has genius, and that his natural gifts can never be communicated to me. Yet still, as it is, I have learned much from him. All my best ideas have come from him, and that very picture of mine was suggested by him. I'll never take the prize while he is here."

At such an outburst of generous feeling all present were deeply moved, and there was not a little confusion. Sagredo pressed the hand of his friend in deep emotion.

"No, dear friend," said he, "you shall not sacrifice yourself in this way. Your picture deserves the prize. You must take it. We can have other chances of competing in future years."

As he spoke, Titian came up.

"Yes," said he, "Pezaro; Sagredo is right. You must take the prize. Your picture is the best here, and the prize must be yours, and yours only. It is yours fairly, justly, and honorably. But more than this is yours, Pezaro; for no prize that man can offer is a fitting reward for your chivalrous friendship, your splendid self-abnegation, and your noble generosity. Take the prize, Pezaro, and let the world learn from you that there is one painter at least who is free from envy and jealousy — that curse of artists."

As he spoke these last words, Titian fixed his eyes on Urso. The latter quailed before his glance, and looked away. Shortly afterwards he retired from the room.

And so Pezaro took the prize.

As for Sagredo, this mishap did not greatly harm him. It elicited general sympathy, and made his merits better known. Other occasions came when his works were displayed and his genius recognized.

As for Urso, he did not remain long in Venice. For it was found that he had made the acquaintance of the janitor, and used to visit him under various pretexts. Moreover, on the evening of the exhibition he had persuaded the janitor to let him see the pictures. Permission was granted, and thus circumstances all pointed towards him as the only possible author of this foul deed. Urso's own acts confirmed the general suspicion, for shortly afterwards he quietly retired from Venice, and was never heard of again.

CHAPTER XIX.

Vernon visits the Police. — Strange Tidings. — Off to the Hotel Zeno. — Disappointment. — Clive and David find out the Error of their Ways.

AFTER their return, Vernon went at once to the Police Bureau to make inquiries about Miss Lee. Thus far he had received no satisfaction; and now he had the same ill fortune. He thought this very strange, and it seemed still stranger when, on further questioning, he could obtain no information whatever. Either the Venetian police were unwilling to talk of their proceedings to outsiders, or else they had utterly failed in the business for which he wished their aid. The latter seemed to Vernon to be the true state of the case, and he began to feel deep vexation at the uselessness of the aid which he had offered to Gracie.

While he was talking, there came in the official with whom Frank and Uncle Moses had come in contact. Some of the words in the conversation attracted his attention, and he came towards Vernon.

"Pardon, signor," said he; "but are you the

gentleman who has been requesting us to make inquiries after Miss Lee?"

" Yes."

" At Verona?"

" Yes."

" Well, do you know that there are others here who have been requesting our aid in search of this same Miss Lee?"

" Others!" said Vernon, in surprise.

" Yes. Do you know them?"

" No."

" They have been here several times. I wonder that you have not met them. But Venice is a difficult place for friends to meet, unless they know one another's movements. At any rate, these others assert that Miss Lee is in Venice."

" In Venice!"

" O, yes: they know it."

" Is it possible! And did they ask you to search after her? and have you found her?" asked Vernon, eagerly.

The official shook his head.

" We have found nothing. She cannot be in Venice. All that is known of her is, that she was last at the Hotel Zeno."

" The Hotel Zeno!" cried Vernon, in fresh surprise. " When?"

" The day before yesterday."

" The day before yesterday?" said Vernon. " That was impossible, for I was there myself, and saw nothing of her, and that was the very time when I first came here to ask your aid."

" Nevertheless," said the official, in his most impressive tone, " Miss Lee was at the Hotel Zeno the day before yesterday. She came there in company with two boys. After staying there, she left with the same two boys. These others, who have been making inquiries here, are more eager to find the boys than they are to find Miss Lee."

Upon the receipt of this astonishing information, Vernon was at first quite .confounded. But at length the facts of the case began to be evident. He saw plainly that these strangers, who had come in search of the boys, could be no others than Uncle Moses, with Frank and Bob, of whom he had heard often enough from his young guests, and that the boys whom they were seeking must be David and Clive; while the Miss Lee, for whom they inquired, must be Gracie herself, and not the aunt. What they could want with Gracie he did not exactly know; but of this he did not think. Two great facts were before him, one being that Gracie's aunt was still among the missing, and the other that Uncle Moses had hurried to Venice in pursuit of Clive and David. For the first time he understood the position of these two, and saw that they were regarded by their anxious uncle as runaways.

" Then you have not found these boys."

" No," said the official.

Upon this Vernon explained to him the facts of the case.

"Where are these people staying?" he asked.

"At the Hotel Zeno."

"Very well; I will go there at once with the boys, and they will be able to join their friends. There need be no more trouble about that."

"You are not acquainted with the old man, then?" said the official.

"No."

"They have had great trouble to-day," continued the official, "and will be glad to see you, if you go with the boys."

"Trouble? What kind of trouble?" asked Vernon.

The official went on to tell them about the arrest of Bob. Vernon listened with a mixture of surprise and merriment.

"But I did not know that swimming in the canal is against the laws," said he. "I swim in the canals constantly, whenever I have time to go out to Lido, or some other place."

"O, it's not against the laws; but on the Grand Canal no one can swim after a certain hour, and this boy was beyond the time. Besides, when the men chased him, they at first intended only to warn him, but he gave them so much trouble that they arrested him."

There was nothing more to be learned now; so Vernon returned home.

Gracie came to meet him, looking at him with anxious inquiry.

Vernon sadly shook his head.

" What ! " said she. " Have you heard nothing ? "

" Not a word."

At this tears started into Gracie's eyes.

" Cheer up," said Vernon, tenderly. " I'll go myself to-morrow. We can arrange all about it to-night. I'm of the opinion that the police have neglected the business. I'm sure, if they had tried, they might have learned something. They could, at least, have found out whether she is in Verona or not. But they know nothing at all, and it is just as if they had not sent any messenger. And I'm half inclined to think that they did not. The fact is, it was my own stupidity. I should have feed them well, but I forgot: and then I haven't shaken off my American ideas about feeing. It doesn't come natural to us. We never fee any one in America, and it takes a long time for one to get into the habit of it here ; besides, when one is at all occupied with other thoughts, he forgets all his new feeing habit. But don't look so sad," continued Vernon, in an anxious voice. " I'll go myself. I'll do all that is possible, and I won't come back to you again until I bring your aunt with me."

At this a smile broke through Gracie's tears, and she murmured some low, sweet words of thanks.

After this, Vernon hastened to acquaint Clive and David with the extraordinary news that Uncle Moses, with Frank and Bob, was here in Venice, and had been seeking after them. He also told the story of Bob's adventure with the police. This intelligence filled David and Clive with varied feelings. Astonishment at finding Uncle Moses here was followed by the sudden discovery that they had acted towards him in a way that seemed both inconsiderate and heartless. The remorse which they felt for this was, however, much mitigated by the idea of Bob's bath; for they saw only the humorous side of this adventure, and did not imagine what anguish of soul it had caused to all concerned.

But the one thought now was, that Uncle Moses was here in Venice; and their one impulse was, to hurry immediately to the Hotel Zeno. All could then be explained; and he, in his joy at finding them, would forgive them all. Vernon also was anxious to see Uncle Moses, for it seemed to him that his inquiries after Miss Lee indicated some knowledge, on his part, of Gracie's aunt. It was quite possible that he had met her, and while seeking after Clive and David, had also included Gracie in the search.

This was all explained to Gracie, who felt sure that it must be so. Uncle Moses, she thought, could not have mentioned her to the police, unless he had met with her aunt, and had been commissioned by her to do so. And thus it became highly necessary, for many reasons, to see Uncle Moses as soon as possible.

Taking Clive and David with him, Vernon now went to the Hotel Zeno. They all expected to see the objects of their search, and were full of hope and pleasant anticipation; but these feelings were in an instant dispelled by the first answer which they received to their eager question.

They had gone — they had left the city.

"Gone? Where?"

"To Verona."

"Verona!"

The disappointment was, indeed, great and hard to bear. All the self-reproach and remorse that their conduct might cause were now felt by Clive and David, as they stood and stared at each other in consternation.

The landlord went on to explain all. He said that they had arrived on the previous day, and had inquired anxiously about Clive and David; that they had then gone to the police to get assistance towards finding them; that the old man was very sad, but the boys were indifferent. Then he alluded to Bob's arrest, and described the anxiety of Uncle Moses and Frank; and then said that after Bob's deliverance they had all hurried away, still hoping to find Clive and David, and thinking that Verona would be the most likely place in which to discover them.

The landlord's information completed the dejection of Clive and David. They now understood all. They perceived that Uncle Moses had been tormented by his anxiety ever since they had left him: that he had left Florence before the time mentioned, and must have followed close on their track, as he had been only one day behind them. How he had managed to track them was not a difficult question to answer. He had heard of them at the different hotels, and had tracked them to the Hotel Zeno. There he had been at fault; and then thinking that they were still wandering about, he had hurried away to Verona. Formerly they had been accustomed to laugh at the anxiety of Uncle Moses: but now, knowing as they did his gentle and affectionate nature, they were shocked at the thought of the misery which must have been inflicted upon him by their own hasty and inconsiderate acts. They saw that while they had been intent only upon their own enjoyment, and had been giving themselves up, without a thought of others, to their own selfish pleasure, their poor dear Uncle Moses had been following after them from place to place, seeking them, but finding them not. What was worst of all, they saw that even now he was far away at Verona; there, as elsewhere, carrying on his search after them, but only to meet with fresh disappointments, worse than any which he had hitherto encountered. They felt now as if they could never forgive themselves;

and as if they could never rest until they had hurried after him, and begged his forgiveness on their knees.

There was nothing more to be learned at the Hotel Zeno, and so they all returned. Vernon was deeply disappointed, because he had hoped to obtain some news to bring back to Gracie, with which he might cheer her; while Clive and David were both disappointed and distressed. Fortunately for Vernon, he had forborne to say anything to Gracie, before starting, about his hope of hearing from Uncle Moses some news of her aunt; and as she had expected nothing, she could not be disappointed.

On reaching the house, Vernon repeated to Gracie his promise that he would go himself in search of her aunt; and this seemed to give her consolation. Besides, she was drawn away from her own troubles by the sight of the great distress of Clive and David. She tried to console them, and spoke to them words of hope and encouragement.

"How funny it all seems!" said she. "We were all runaways — all three of us. It's the old proverb — Birds of a feather flock together. I didn't know that you were runaways, but I must have felt it; and that must have been the reason why my heart warmed towards you. Misery loves company, as another proverb says; so, boys, the best thing that we can do is to sit in a corner together, and have a good cry. Of course you won't cry, because you're so proud; but I'm not proud a bit, and I mean to cry my eyes out."

"If you are going to Verona," said Clive, "may we not go with you?"

"What good would that do?" asked Vernon.

"Why, we should meet Uncle Moses."

"Do you suppose that he will be at Verona by the time that you would get there?"

"Why not?"

"Well, I've been thinking of that, and it seems to me that he would not stay there longer than he could help. He arrived there this evening. He has gone to the two chief hotels, the only places where he would be likely to find you, or you would be likely to stay. He has found that you are not there. So he has already concluded that you are not at Verona, and is, perhaps, just now debating with Frank and Bob about the most likely course that you could have taken in your erratic wanderings. And Uncle Moses is all at sea; but there is a fierce argument between Frank and Bob; one of whom, Frank, is for going back to Florence, and waiting till they hear from you; while Bob is eager to go on to Milan."

At this fancy sketch, Clive and David gave a sickly smile. They were not in the humor for fun. Their distress was too deep.

"But we could go with you," said David, "and find them, wherever they are."

"No," said Vernon. "Let me go alone. Your best place is here. I'll find Uncle Moses, and send him here to you. You've been wandering about long enough. Stay here by all means, in one fixed place, till you hear from him or from me. That's your safest plan."

"But wouldn't it be well to telegraph?"

"O, most excellent, if you only knew where to telegraph. But where? that is the question. To Verona? But by to-morrow morning they'll be on the wing. To Milan? But they may go to Florence. To Florence? But they may come here to Venice. You see it's all uncertain, and the only thing you can do now is, to stand still and let them come to you."

It seemed very hard to Clive and David, yet Vernon's words were unanswerable, and so they concluded to leave all to him, and do just what he said.

CHAPTER XX.

The End of Happiness. — The cheerful Vernon. — Gracie's Resolution. — A lost Day. — Verona. — Inquiries. — The right Track. — The Amphitheatre at Sunset. — An interesting Conversation.

AND thus all their happiness had come to an end. There were no more pleasant expeditions about the wonderful city; no more seasons of dreamy enjoyment; no more wanderings through long galleries, or under lofty cathedral arches. All this had come to an end, and they all had something to think of which was far different from Venetian stories.

That evening was of itself enough to show the greatness of the change that had taken place. There was no chance for Vernon to exhibit his pictures, and no one asked him to read any of his stories. He tried to speak in a cheerful way to his guests, but his words had no effect; and Gracie on the one hand, and David and Clive on the other, found it impossible to rouse themselves from the deep gloom into which they had fallen.

Still Vernon persisted in his well-meant efforts to cheer up his melancholy guests, and he directed his attention more particularly towards Gracie.

"I'm quite sure," said he, " that the police have done nothing. It was all owing to my own unfortunate absence of mind. I was so engrossed with other things that I really forgot all about the all-important fee. Nobody in all Italy will think of doing anything without a preliminary fee. It's the same all over Europe. In America it's totally different, and it's hard for an American to get into the way of it. Aside from its strangeness, there seems to an American something degrading about it ; and so, you see, it's a long time before one can grow to have one's wits about him in this respect. O, yes, I'm quite certain that this is the whole trouble. That accounts for their indifference, their ignorance, their assurances of pretended messages and messengers, with their absolute inaction. They're not humbugs ; they are merely waiting for their fee. At all events, what's done can't be undone ; and so I'll go myself. The Venetian police shan't get any fees from me. I'll go to Verona, and search for myself, and I'll be hanged if I don't believe that I'll do better than any police agent, fee and all.

" Now, as to your aunt, I really don't think that you need worry so much. It's only fifty-six hours since you left her. It was the day before yesterday. Fifty-six hours ! The day before yesterday ! What's that ? Why, it's nothing at all. You speak as though fifty-six months had passed. The time seems long to you, I dare say," continued Vernon, reproachfully. " I dare say it seems like fifty-six

18

years; but to me it seems like fifty-six minutes. At any rate, you have only lost your aunt for a few hours. She's in Verona now, you may be sure. She's waiting quietly there till you come back. I dare say she is a little worried about you, for fear that you have come to harm; but as for herself, she's all right. She's at the Hotel de la Tour, or the Hotel Deux Tours — one or the other; it don't matter which. All she wants is to know that you are well; and as you know yourself that you are well, why worry about your aunt? I mean to go to Verona, and go straight to the Hotel de la Tour, and ask for Miss Lee. I shall see her at once. I shall tell her how I found you, ask her to take my arm, and we shall come back by return train. She will be here by evening, and you will wonder how in the world you managed to make such a heap of trouble about a mere trifle."

These were brave words. Gracie smiled, but the smile did not hide the anxiety which still remained within her heart, undiminished.

On the following morning, Vernon was preparing for his departure, when Gracie informed him that she had a request to make.

"I've been awake all night," said Gracie, "and I'm so awfully worried that I cannot endure it; and I cannot bear to stay here any longer, and I've been speaking to your mother about it, and I want to go to Verona myself."

"With me!" said Vernon, as a flush of joy overspread his face.

"Yes," said Gracie, "and I've been talking with your mother, and she has offered to go with me; and I thought I'd mention it to you, so as to know whether there is anything to prevent it, or if it will interfere with your search."

"Interfere!" cried Vernon, in the utmost joy. "Interfere! Why, it will be the very thing. And will mother really go?"

"She said — as I am so worried — that she would go with me; and you know the boys can stay here all the same, or go with us."

"The boys — O, they must stay here," said Vernon. "The best thing for them now is to stay in this one place and wait. But you! and will you really come with me? and will mother come? O, that will be more than I dared hope for. And I shan't have to leave you, after all, and we can make our search together."

Vernon was quite beside himself with joy at this proposal. Gracie had made it out of her deep anxiety; but to Vernon it seemed the highest happiness. He loved so much to be with Gracie that this journey had seemed almost intolerable; but now the dreaded parting need not take place, for she, too, was coming.

Clive and David heard of this, but they had nothing to say. They both felt guilty; and as they had sinned through wilfulness and thoughtlessness, they now felt ready to resign thought and will to another. They accepted the situation, therefore, with resignation, and in silence, and tried to console themselves with the hope that it would be all for the best.

This new arrangement, however, made very serious alterations in Vernon's plans. For Mrs. Vernon was a quiet lady, who travelled but little, and so hated to move from her home that the prospect of such a thing never failed to fill her with confusion. On the present occasion, the journey before her, short though it was, served to completely bewilder her. She was reduced to a state of nervous trepidation and fidgety anxiety about her preparations. The train was to leave at ten o'clock; and in her eagerness to make ready she utterly broke down from overwork and nervousness. Then she tried to rally; and then new trouble arose from her own weakness, and she implored her son to go without her. But Vernon would not; for upon her going depended Gracie's going, and he would not leave now without her sweet companionship. There were two other trains, one at three, and another at seven: but for the remainder of that day Mrs. Vernon was unable to travel, and the end of it all was, that they had to postpone it until the following day.

They had thus lost a whole day; but Gracie felt consoled at the thought that she herself would, after all, be able to go, and Vernon did not care for the loss of days, so long as Gracie was with him. Fortunately Mrs. Vernon succeeded in overcoming her nervousness, and in effecting her preparations, so that on the following day they all left by the ten o'clock train. David and Clive went with them to the railway station, and bade them farewell with melancholy faces. They knew that they had done wrong, and that they were now suffering the penalty of such wrong doing, and could only hope that Uncle Moses would be restored to them, in which case each one inwardly vowed that he would for the future do exactly as Uncle Moses said, no matter how much it might interfere with their private inclinations.

The journey proved so pleasant to Vernon and to Gracie that both were sorry when it came to an end. Vernon was happy because Gracie was by his side, and Gracie was happy because she felt as though she was with every mile drawing nearer to her aunt. All her anxiety had now passed away; or else it had been postponed to some more convenient season. Poor Mrs. Vernon, who had come as chaperon, had not slept during the past night; and she made amends for this by sleeping throughout the whole journey, which left Vernon free to say many things that he might not have said if she had been awake.

At length they arrived at Verona, and went to the Hotel de la Tour, where they put up. Here Vernon at once asked if any one had been stopping there by the name of Lee — Signora Lee — an American lady.

No such person had been stopping there.

This was very disheartening information; but Vernon was prepared for this, and went off at once to the Hotel Deux Tours. Here, however, he was equally unsuccessful, and found that nothing was known about any such person. After this he went to many other hotels and lodging-houses, thinking no place too unlikely for an inexperienced stranger to stop at: but in spite of this he had the deep mortification to find his comprehensive search of no avail whatever, for he could not discover the slightest trace of the party in question. So the end of it all was, that he had to come back to his friends with the sad confession that thus far he had been baffled. This intelligence gave the deepest pain to Gracie, and it was evident that she was now thoroughly alarmed.

"I will see the police," said Vernon. "This time I will go with them myself. We will telegraph all over Italy. Something must and shall be found out."

He now went to have another conversation with the landlord.

"Have you had any ladies here lately?" he asked.

"Yes; a lady was here; she went away this morning. She was a foreigner, a Russian, I think; but she spoke English."

"O, she spoke English — did she?"

"Yes; and some friends of hers came here. They were English. She went away with them."

" English friends. Ah!" said Vernon; " and you think she was Russian."

The thing had very little interest for him now, but he asked once more.

" What was the lady's name ? "

" Madame Missoli," said the landlord.

" Madame Missoli ! I never heard of that name," said Vernon. It was plain to him that this lady was of no interest to him. Thus far he had forgotten about Uncle Moses and the boys, but now it occurred to him to make inquiries after them. One of the objects of his search had failed, but he might try, after all, to seek out the other. So he asked, —

" Have you had any Americans here lately ? "

" Americans ? " said the landlord. " Yes. We had some. They came the day before yesterday. I don't know whether they were Americans or English. They were the ones who went away with Madame Missoli. An old man and two boys."

At this Vernon eagerly interrupted him. An old man and two boys ! Evidently they were Uncle Moses and Frank and Bob. Further questions made this certain, and all doubt was driven away by the landlord repeating their names.

With this there came another discovery. The name Missoli : it explained itself. It was the Italian version of Miss Lee. How stupid of him not to perceive this before ! Yes. It must be the missing lady ; and somehow or other Uncle Moses and the boys had made her acquaintance, and they had gone away together. He now asked the landlord to describe the personal appearance of Madame Missoli, and he found that it accorded perfectly with Gracie's description of her aunt.

" Where did they go?" he asked, eagerly, at length, when his last doubt had vanished.

" To Venice."

" Venice? And when?"

" This morning," said the landlord.

" Do you know where they intended to put up?"

" O, yes: it was the Hotel Zeno."

Vernon was now completely overwhelmed by all this sudden and unexpected rush of good news. There was nothing further to ask or to do. The only thing left now was to go back to Venice as fast as possible. So he left the landlord abruptly, and hurried to tell the good news to Gracie. In a few words all was made known; and Gracie was lifted out of the depths of despair to joy and hope. But there was one drawback yet. To go back to Venice that day was not possible. Vernon's search had taken up much time. The last train had gone, and they would have to wait until the following day. Gracie therefore was forced to restrain her impatience, and content herself with the prospect that now lay before her.

There was an hour or two of daylight still before them, and Vernon proposed that they should go out and see the city. Mrs. Vernon excused herself on the ground of fatigue; but Gracie was glad to go, and the two set forth. The load which for a whole day had pressed so heavily on Gracie's mind was now removed, and she resumed all her usual gayety and sprightliness. All seemed fair and bright. She felt certain of meeting with her aunt. It needed only one day more, and the painful separation would be ended. She also very naturally felt as if Vernon had done all this, and amid all her sprightliness there was evident in her manner the tenderness of gratitude.

They walked about the city. They saw its ruins, its cathedral, its public places, and at length found themselves in the grand old amphitheatre. Climbing up the steps, they seated themselves, and looked around upon the scene. The sight which met their eyes was an impressive one, and one which was not soon to be forgotten. The sun was low in the west, and the arena was wrapped in gloom; but the eastern circle of seats in the upper tiers was all crimson in its glowing rays. Their view was bounded by the walls of the amphitheatre, and they sat for some time in silence.

"I'm glad that you are happy," said Vernon; "but I'm afraid I shall be sad enough to-morrow. The arrival of your aunt will put an end to all our wanderings about Venice. And they were so delightful!"

"They were very pleasant," said Gracie, in a low voice. "And I'm sure I hope we shall see more of Venice, and that you will be at leisure, Mr. Vernon."

"At leisure!" said Vernon. "I shall have nothing but leisure as long as you are in Venice. And you are expecting your uncle, too."

"Yes," said Gracie, in a low voice. "He was to be in Venice on the fourth. This is the sixth. He ought to be there now, I should think; but if not, why, we can wait."

"Won't I do?" asked Vernon, very abruptly.

"You!" said Gracie, in surprise.

"Yes," said Vernon. "Won't you let me be your uncle? your guardian? anything? You see how it is. I can't live without you, Gracie. You must see — how — how — how dearly I — I love you;" and as he said this, his hand closed around that of Gracie, which did not withdraw itself. "O, Gracie," he continued, "I cannot bear to have you go away and leave me. You won't — will you? You will stay with me — won't you? You will be my own Gracie — won't you, as long as you live?"

What little Gracie said to all this need not be repeated here. Suffice it to say, that it must have been quite satisfactory; for when they returned to the hotel Vernon's face was radiant with joy.

PRIVATE AMPHITHEATRICALS. — Page 282.

CHAPTER XXI.

The mournful Uncle Moses. — Marius among the Ruins of Carthage. — Uncle Moses startled. — A new Acquaintance.

MEANWHILE Uncle Moses, with Frank and Bob, had arrived at Verona, as has been said. They put up at the Hotel de la Tour. Here, first of all, they asked after Clive and David. Nothing was known about them. Then they made inquiries about a lady named Lee ; but here, too, they were equally unsuccessful. Then they went off to the Hotel Deux Tours, another establishment which contends with the Hotel de la Tour for the honor of being the first in Verona. The latter, however, makes a greater bid for English travel, and has a more sounding name, since its full title is Hotel de la Tour de Londres. But their search at the Hotel Deux Tours was as unsuccessful as the search at the Hotel de la Tour, and they returned somewhat disconsolate, and passed the night.

"I'll tell you, Uncle Moses," said Frank on the following day, "what we had better do. We ought to go about and see all the sights of Verona. If the boys are here, we shall be certain to find them, for they, too, will be going about sight-seeing."

To this proposal Uncle Moses had no objections to make : and as he preferred being with the boys to staying at the hotel, he accompanied them.

Going along the main street, they came to a square which was used as a market-place, and contained many stalls, where all sorts of fruits and vegetables were exposed for sale, the venders being chiefly old women. At one end of it stood a stately palace. On referring to their guide-books they found that this was in ancient days the Forum of the city.

Leaving this, they turned down a street, and before long they found themselves in front of a strange-looking wall which ran across the way. It was about fifty feet high, and there were two gates in it, and a number of windows. It had an unmistakable look of Roman workmanship, and on referring to the guide-book they found that it was part of an ancient work raised by the Emperor Constantine. As a relic of the past, it was, undoubtedly, interesting, although in itself it possessed but little beauty. Proceeding still farther, they turned down another street, and all at once came full in view of the greatest curiosity of Verona, and one of the most interesting monuments of ancient Rome now in existence. This was the famous Amphitheatre, which, in point of size, ranks next to the Coliseum of Rome, while in preservation it is far superior to all other similar remains. They went towards this, and examined it closely. The outer wall was all gone, except a fragment three stories in height, raised on arches one above the other. The rest of the building was only two stories high, and seemed much dilapidated. But when they had entered and looked upon the interior, they were filled with astonishment. They expected to behold a scene of ruin like that of the Coliseum, instead of which they found everything in a state of preservation almost perfect. All around extended the vast circles of seats rising one behind the other far on high, capable still of holding a multitude as large as those which once assembled here, in olden days, to see the gladiatorial combats. The cause of this preservation is the wisdom of the Veronese government. In past ages the temples and towers of antiquity had been demolished in all directions for building materials, and nearly all the outer wall of the Amphitheatre had been appropriated in the same way. The Veronese government interfered in time to prevent further destruction, and snatched the grand old edifice from the ruin that menaced it. The rows of seats, the arena, the vomitories, the inner chambers, the rooms of the gladiators, the vivaria, all are in good preservation; and if the ghosts of the ancient inhabitants could revisit the glimpses of the moon, they would find one spot, at least, which would be perfectly familiar. Even in mod-

ern times this building has been used; and in the
year 1849, in particular, it was the scene of a grand
display, when the spectators were as numerous as
in ancient times, and when the seat of honor was
held by one who claims to be the direct represen-
tative of the Roman emperors, — the Kaisar (Cæsar), — whose forefathers had called themselves
Kaisars of the Roman Empire, until Napoleon
forced them to adopt the humbler title of Kaisar
of Austria.

They all sat down here for some time, and at
length Frank and Bob proposed to go farther.

"Where do you want to go?" asked Uncle
Moses, wearily.

"O, anywhere," said Frank. "There's a Cathedral."

"O, well, don't go far away. Frank, I trust to
you. Don't let Bob get into trouble. I'll sit here
a while, and when I'm rested I'll go back to the
hotel. Don't be late, and don't get into trouble.
I'd rayther go with you; but I ain't so spry as I'd
like to be, an' as I don't want to spile your fun, why,
I'll have to let you go without me."

Uncle Moses spoke very mournfully, and the boys
felt sad at leaving him; but Frank was anxious to
search the city, and still hoped to come upon the
track of Clive and David. So they promised him
solemnly not to go away for any distance, and to
be back in good time. With this they left, and
Uncle Moses was alone.

Thus Uncle Moses remained there, seated in the old Amphitheatre, like Marius amid the ruins of Carthage. It's the best place for me, he thought, sadly. I'll be an old ruin soon myself. His mournful feelings were too much for him. The anxiety which he had endured ever since the departure of David and Clive had made him weak in mind and body, and the failure to find them at Verona was a heavy blow. Thus far he had always succeeded in keeping on their track : but now they were altogether lost, and he could not think where next to go. So he sat there on the steps of the ancient Amphitheatre, with his head bowed down, and his face buried in his hands.

Suddenly he was roused by the touch of a light hand on his shoulder. He started up, expecting to see Frank or Bob. To his surprise it was neither. It was a stranger, and the stranger was a lady; a lady of mature age, with gentle and refined features, whereon much sadness was visible. She was standing and looking at him wistfully and eagerly. As for Uncle Moses, he jumped up to his feet, and stared at her without a single word.

"Will you pardon me, sir," said the lady, "for intruding? but I am in great distress, and this is my only excuse. I happened to hear at the hotel that some strangers had come who were Americans. I hurried down to see them. I saw you and the dear boys who are with you, and heard you speak. I was about to speak to you, but you all went out. But I was in such a fever of anxiety that I followed you, and have just come here. I am in great distress. I have met with a great misfortune. I am all alone here, among strangers, and I want help."

At this, all Uncle Moses' feelings were stirred up to their lowest depths, and all the sympathies of his generous nature were aroused in behalf of the gentle lady who came with such a pitiable appeal.

"O, madam," said he, "I'll do anythin'—anythin' in the wide world, if I can."

He held out his hand, and affectionately pressed that of the lady, to show his sympathy.

"O, thank you, sir," said the lady; "I'll tell you how I am situated. I came from Boston. My name is Miss Lee."

"Miss Lee!" cried Uncle Moses, in amazement.

"Yes," said Miss Lee, surprised at his look and tone.

"Miss Lee," cried Uncle Moses again; "and weren't you in Venice? and didn't you meet my two boys? and have you come to tell me about them? O, if you can tell me anything, do, do, for I'm heart-broken."

Miss Lee shook her head mournfully. "I don't understand you," said she. "I haven't been in Venice, and I haven't seen any boys, except those dear lads that you have with you. They are not lost—are they? for they have just left you; or have you lost any others."

"Others? O, yes, marm," said Uncle Moses,
with a groan; "they left me at Florence, and went
to Venice. I tracked them there, and couldn't find
them. But they told me at the hotel that they had
been there with a Miss Lee, and had gone away.
I understood that they had gone to Verona; and
that's why I came here."

Miss Lee clasped Uncle Moses' arm with both
her hands.

"What's that?" she said, eagerly; "Miss Lee?
When did your boys go to Venice?"

"Wal, as nigh as I can cal'late, they left Padua
for Venice the day before yesterday."

"In the morning?" asked Miss Lee, with intense
eagerness.

"Yes, 'm."

"Then they must have been in the same train.
They've found her, and she's safe. O, I thank
Heaven! O, sir, what a load you have taken off
my mind!"

"Wal, won't you try and take a little of the load
off my mnid?" said Uncle Moses. "Who is ' her? '
Who did they meet? Is there any other Miss Lee
but you?"

'O, it's my niece — Gracie."

"Your niece, Gracie!" said Uncle Moses, in a
strange tone.

"O, yes; and I'll tell you all about it. O, sir,
how glad I am that I've met with you! Heaven

has sent you here in answer to my prayer; and I'm sure we shall be able to help one another."

At this flattering mention of himself as a heavenly messenger, a smile broke out upon the rueful visage of Uncle Moses like sunshine, and all the clouds were rapidly dispelled. There was something, also, in what Miss Lee said that reassured him. It showed that others had lost their youthful charges as well as himself, and that things were not so bad, after all. Besides, he felt compelled to take up the attitude of consoler and adviser to this forlorn lady, and therefore he had to rouse himself from his own despondency, so as to infuse hope into her.

"O, come," said he, "an' set right down here, an' tell me all about it. We'll be able to get on to their trail, an' hunt 'em down. So they're all together — air they? my boys and your gal. Well, that is cur'ous, too. I can't account for it, no how."

As Uncle Moses said these words, he seated himself again, and motioned to Miss Lee to take a seat beside him. This that lady did, and then began to pour forth the story of her woes.

She had left home in company with her brother, his wife, and some other friends. Gracie was under her special charge, and had been sent to Europe for the benefit of her health. After various wanderings they had reached Geneva, and here the whole party remained for some time. Her brother and his wife then wished to go to Italy; but Miss Lee did not feel able to endure the fatigues of rapid travel and sight-seeing; so an arrangement was made, by which she should remain in Geneva for another month, and then meet them in Venice. The brother then departed with his wife and friends for Marseilles, and had written from Genoa, Naples, Rome, and Florence. On the receipt of the last letter, Miss Lee had started for Venice with Gracie, and nothing of importance had occurred until the eventful morning of their sepaation.

"But why did you stay here?" asked Uncle Moses. "Why didn't you go right straight on after her?"

Miss Lee sighed.

"Why," said she, "when the train went off and left me, I was so terrified and bewildered that I could think of nothing. I couldn't speak a word of the language, and didn't know what to do. I thought that Gracie would come back to me, and my only thought was to wait here for her. So I waited at the depot till the return train came, and when I saw she was not in it, I was quite overwhelmed. Still I hoped that she would come back; and so I put up at the Hotel de la Tour, and thought I would wait 'till the next day. I went to the depot on the next day, but she was not there. Then I began to be afraid that something had happened. The worst of it was, I had staid here so long that I could not think of going away; and my only hope has been that Gracie, after all, would come back to me. But, amid it all, there was the dreadful fear that the poor child had met with some frightful misfortune. And so these two days have been full of misery, and I do not know what I should have done if I hadn't met with you. And now I feel as if all my troubles were over, for you can help me to find Gracie; and from what you say she must be with your boys."

"O, yes, 'm," said Uncle Moses, in a tone of confidence that was very unlike his recent dejection; "we'll find 'em. They're all together somewhars, an' we'll get on their track an' bring 'em all back like so many prodigal sons. On'y it's a leetle hard to tell whar to begin. I've come here in search of 'em, but can't find any signs of 'em at all. I don't know what else to do but to hand the business over to the police."

"The police!" said Miss Lee, in a tone of horror. "O, would you dare to go near them? The only fear I have had is, that poor Gracie may have fallen into their hands."

"Why, what harm would they do?" asked Uncle Moses.

"Put her into their dungeons," said Miss Lee, in a tremulous voice.

Uncle Moses shuddered. At the same time he felt it incumbent on him to administer consolation to his companion; and so he struggled against his fears, and strove to speak with boldness and confident assurance. The result was, that his language towards Miss Lee was strikingly like that of Frank towards himself, and the very act of talking boldly served to revive his own feeble courage.

"O, then," said Miss Lee, at last, "so you think the police here are not what they used to be."

"Not a mite," said Uncle Moses; "they're polite, civil, sensible, and humane. They wouldn't harm a fly. It's all a mistake to think that they air any different from the police to home. Why, look at me. I've been to see 'em, at Venice, and got 'em to help me with my boys. An' so I think we had better get their help here."

CHAPTER XXII.

Wonderful Change in Uncle Moses. — The new Friend. — New Resolves. — Application to the Police.

NOTHING that had occurred to Uncle Moses, during the whole course of his travels in Italy, gave him such pure delight as his meeting with Miss Lee. He liked her gentle face and soft voice: he was touched by her appeal for assistance and her trust in him. Above all, he was most affected by her timidity, and her nervous terrors as to imaginary evils. Her misfortunes had been similar to his own. They each could sympathize with the other. It was delicious to Uncle Moses to meet with some one who was a greater coward than himself, and it was most flattering to his self-esteem, for he had to take up the attitude of a superior being towards her.

"My dear Miss Lee," said Uncle Moses. taking her hand in an affectionate way and pressing it tenderly, — "my dear Miss Lee, don't you go on an' give yourself any more trouble ; don't fret or worry. I'll take care of you. Leave all to me. Thar ain't a mite of danger — not a mite. We'll find 'em all safe an' sound — my boys, Clive and

David, an' your gal, Gracie. I see how it is: they've all got acquainted in the train, an' gone on to Venice. They all went to the same hotel, an' your Gracie was the Miss Lee that the landlord spoke of. I dar say they're in Venice yet, an' hev merely gone to lodgin's. I heard that there was a Miss Lee in Verona, an' thought it was the same Miss Lee that the boys had met with. I asked the police to send here. Did you not hear from them?"

"Not a word," said Miss Lee. "But how did you hear that there was a Miss Lee in Verona? That seems strange."

"Why, the police told me that ther'd been people there askin' them to send to Verona for you."

Miss Lee's face brightened up at this.

"Then my friends are there in Venice," said she. "It must be my brother Henry. But how did he know that I was at Verona? No doubt Gracie told him. They've met — of course. I understand it all now. Gracie's met her uncle and gone to his hotel, and the boys have gone with him."

"They're not at any hotel in Venice," said Uncle Moses. "The police hunted everywhere."

"O, well, they're at some lodgings."

"O, the fact is," said Uncle Moses, cheerily, "they're all right. There ain't a mite of danger — not a mite; so don't you bother your head any longer about it. Cheer up, marm, an' put a good face on it. Why, look at me; I've lost two, an' you've only lost one. Wal, do I mourn an' lament? Do I despair? Not a mite. Why, at this moment I'm as merry as a cricket. I know the boys air safe, an' that we'll meet 'em all the minute we go back to Venice."

At this moment the conversation was interrupted by the arrival of Frank and Bob. So deeply interested had Uncle Moses and Miss Lee been in their conversation, that they heard nothing of the approach of the new comers, and Uncle Moses had gone on talking in a way that indicated the greatest boldness and confidence. Frank and Bob heard his last words, and were full of amazement. Was it possible that this could be their Uncle Moses? What a change had come over him! They had left him weak, feeble, crushed, and despairing, without spirit enough to say a word; they found him strong, spirited, animated, bold, speaking words of hope and confidence. They saw that the strange lady was an American, and could only conclude that Uncle Moses had heard from her good news, which had wrought upon him this great change.

In a few moments all was explained, and the quick wit of Frank made him see at once the full bearing of this unexpected meeting with Miss Lee upon their own business. Uncle Moses stated the conclusions to which he had already come, and then added, —

"So you see, Frank, there ain't a mite of doubt

about it; the boys were in Venice all the time, an'
if we hadn't ben so impatient, we'd have found them
by this time."

By the tone in which Uncle Moses spoke these
words, one would have supposed that he had never
known what it was to be anxious. Frank at once
chimed in with his uncle's altered mood, and finding his occupation of comforter gone, he humbly
asked what he intended to do now.

"Do?" said Uncle Moses. "Why, go back to
Venice."

"Yes, I think that is the best plan," said Frank.
"And when can you start?"

"Why, to-day," said Uncle Moses; "that is, if
Miss Lee is ready."

"When does the next train leave?" asked Miss
Lee.

"In a half an hour," said Frank.

"O, I'm afraid I couldn't get ready by that time,"
said Miss Lee. "You must go without me."

"No," said Uncle Moses; "we must all go together. We'll wait till you are ready. If we separate now, we may never meet again, and may miss
the rest of 'em, too."

"I'm very sorry," said Miss Lee, "to be unable
to go, but I could not pack up in so short a time;
but if you do not mind waiting, why, of course I
shall be deeply grateful."

"Wait? Of course we'll wait," said Uncle Moses.
"Arter all, it ain't goin' to make any difference —

not a mite; an' to go without you won't be a bit
of use. So we'll wait, an' all go together. As
we've suffered together, so shall we rejice together."

"I suppose," said Miss Lee, "there would be no
harm in sending word to Venice, to tell them that
we are here and are coming."

"No harm," said Uncle Moses; "course not.
On'y I'd like to know who to send it to. The
parties who were inquirin' arter you didn't give
their address to me. They left it with the police.
And then none of us knows where Clive, or David,
or your niece may be."

"Wouldn't it be better to get the police here
to send a message to the police in Venice?" said
Frank.

"Course it would," said Uncle Moses. "That's
the very pint I was comin' to. That's our plan.
Let's go right straight off to the police."

"The police!" repeated Miss Lee, with a startled
look.

"Yes," said Uncle Moses. "We'll tell 'em how
it is. Get 'em to send a message to the Venetian
police, who will communicate with your friends;
and at the same time, urge them to look up Clive
and David. I dar say they've found them by this
time, if they railly air in Venice. An' as to tho
police," continued Uncle Moses, directing his remarks to Miss Lee, "don't you go an' give yourself one mite of trouble about that. The police

In the Hands of the Police. — Page 498.

here air no more than the police in Boston. Jest imagine that you air safe at home, an' drop all these superstitious fears about the police. Why, you're as safe here as in Massachusetts. This here's a free government, an' they've got habeas corpus, trial by jury, vote by ballot, an' a free constitution. So what more do you want?"

These words, which greatly re-assured Miss Lee, sounded at once strange and delicious to Frank. He had been using almost the same words during the last few days, to console and re-assure the very same Uncle Moses, who now repeated them so boldly and confidently. He wondered at the change, and could not imagine the cause; yet that change was very pleasant to him, to whom his uncle's deep dejection had been a very sore trial.

They now left the Amphitheatre, and went at once to the police station. Here there was an interpreter, by whose aid they were able to make known their wants. Unfortunately the interpreter's English was rather shaky, and some little misunderstanding arose, which afterwards led to results that for a time were unpleasant.

Frank was the spokesman, as Uncle Moses had greater confidence in his ability to deal with foreigners than in his own. He therefore made known the situation in as few words as possible, not forgetting to bestow a handsome fee, the reception of which at once seemed to stimulate the rather drowsy zeal of the officials.

Frank informed them of the facts of the case, just as they were, and these plain facts were translated in such a way that the officials received a somewhat different impression from that which was intended.

They understood that David, and Clive, and Gracie had all run away from their guardians, and had met somewhere by a preconcerted arrangement, after which they had concealed themselves in Venice, and that the guardians, having just learned of their hiding-place, were anxious that they should be found, and arrested at once, and detained until they should go on to Venice themselves. These guardians were anxious also that it should be done this very day, for fear lest the fugitives might escape them.

This the Verona police promised to do, and that very hour they sent off a telegraphic despatch to the Venetian police, ordering the immediate arrest of the fugitives.

CHAPTER XXIII.

Clive and David. — Unwelcome Visitors. — Arrested. — Hauled to Prison. — The Dungeons of Venice. — Despair of the Captives.

VERNON'S last visit to the Venetian police had made them well acquainted with the fact that he had with him two boys whose uncle he wished to find, and the young lady after whose aunt he had been searching. Acccordingly, when they received the despatch from Verona, it seemed a part of the same business which had been brought before them in various ways and from various quarters during the past few days. It seemed like a summary ending to that business, and it was a thing that lay entirely in their power. They knew perfectly well what Vernon's address was; they knew that the fugitives mentioned in the despatch were all there : and so they proceeded to carry the demand of the Veronese police into execution.

Vernon had gone away with his mother and Gracie. David and Clive had been left, with the strictest instructions to take care of themselves, and not get into any fresh difficulty. These instructions they had received with deep humility, and had promised to obey them to the very letter. After seeing their friends off at the station, they had returned to Vernon's house, and there discussed in a mournful way their situation and prospects. Their pleasant excitement had now all passed away. Sight-seeing could no longer interest them. There was always present before their minds the image of the distracted Uncle Moses, seeking for the run-aways, and finding them not : tracing them in town after town, as far as Venice, only to lose them at last. And now, where had he gone? or what was he proposing to do? To give them up? Impossible. He seemed rather to be entering upon a search which was far away from the right direction, and would only lead to fresh disappointment and renewed anxiety. He had gone to Verona, but might already have left that place ; and although they both longed to join him again, yet they knew not where to go, and could only rely upon Vernon. They reproached themselves most bitterly for their thoughtlessness, and these sad feelings deprived them of all capacity for enjoyment. Venice had now lost all its charms. They were alone in the house, with only the housekeeper and one servant, who could be no company for them. Besides, they missed Vernon, and his mother, and Gracie, whose company had made the past few days so pleasant. All these things combined to make them feel mis-erable enough, and so they returned from the rail-

way station to mope about the house. In this way
they passed the morning.

But youthful minds are elastic, and it is impossible, under ordinary circumstances, for the pressure
of grief to last very long. David and Clive found
themselves gradually rallying; and although they
both preserved an aspect of gloom, still they allowed their thoughts to wander freely over pleasant subjects, and spent some agreeable hours in
turning over pictures, and in reading. At last, David, in his most sepulchral tone, proposed that they
should go to the Piazza of St. Mark, alleging as an
excuse that he had a bad headache, and wanted
some fresh air and exercise. To this proposal
Clive assented in gloomy silence, and so they prepared to start.

Just as they were going down stairs, however,
they found themselves face to face with some policemen, who were coming up. These policemen
looked at them with very significant faces, and before they knew what to think they found themselves
arrested, and heard words in which they detected,
" Prigionieri," " fuggitivi," " arrestovi in nome del
Re," with some others, all of which were intelligible enough even to one who had but a slender acquaintance with the Italian language.

They were detained for some time in the lower
hall, while the police went up to Vernon's apartments. After a time they came back, and David
and Clive were able to make out that they had

gone in search of Signorina Lee, and that they had not been able to find her. In the midst of their perplexity, terror, and dismay, the two boys felt glad indeed that Gracie was safe, out of danger, and that she had not been left behind to share their terrific fate.

Terrific!— that was the word, for indeed to be arrested by the police in any European city is a serious thing; but who can think without a shudder of an arrest by the police of Venice? At any rate, Clive and David could not. All their past knowledge of Venice, all that they had heard from Vernon, and seen with their own eyes, came before their minds. The Venetian police — what a terrible significance was there in that name! What horrors lay in the past history of that police!— a history associated with hideous memories of dungeon, and rack, and agony, and despair. True, the worst of their tortures had been abolished; but the habit of cruelty might be strong; and who could tell what deeds of darkness were still perpetrated by the dread tribunal which now presided over the affairs of this mysterious city!

After a further delay, they were taken to the police boat, and away they knew not where. As they went away they hoped to learn something about the cause of their arrest, but were disappointed. Nothing was said. None of the faces were familiar, and none were at all inviting. They all looked like machines — the soulless instruments of a cruel law. The sight of these grim and silent men made Clive and David sink down into deeper dejection and despair.

At length they reached the police station, and were taken inside. Here they found some officials who regarded them with looks in which there was no trace of softness or pity. Clive roused himself, and asked in English if there was an interpreter to be had; but no notice was taken of his words. Then David, encouraged by Clive's boldness, ventured upon a few Italian words. He looked at one of the officials, who seemed to be the chief, and said, —

"Vogliamo un interpreter. Siamo Americani — e vogliamo vedere il Consule Americano."

This was bad Italian, and spoken with an absurdly foreign accent; yet it was intelligible enough, and David hoped to effect something by it. His hopes, however, were vain. No notice whatever was taken of his words. It was just the same as if they had not been spoken. The officials conversed for a while among themselves, and then one of them beckoned to another. This last took David and Clive by the arms, and led them out of the room and into a long hall, which they traversed, and at length stopped in front of a door. This was opened, and their guide motioned to them to go in. They did so. He then locked the door, and they heard his retreating footsteps as he walked away.

This was the most awful moment in their lives;

20

a moment which far exceeded anything that they had ever known, and which could only be compared, in point of utter horror, to some of those terrific situations which the mind may invent in a nightmare dream. Standing motionless and mute, staring at one another with pallid faces, the two wretched boys saw nothing, and heard nothing, and thought of nothing. Terror had almost taken away their senses. The whole incident of the arrest had been at once so sudden, so terrible, so overwhelming, that they were only conscious of some fearful doom impending over them.

The room was not a dungeon, however, and though somewhat dreary, had nothing in it which of itself might inspire terror. It was a room with plain walls, lighted by a small window that seemed to look out on a court-yard. There were two beds, two chairs, a table, and a wash-stand. There was certainly something cheerless in its aspect, yet, after all, it was a commonplace room enough, and might have belonged to some Italian inn, as well as to the Venetian police.

It was this that at length served to dispel to some extent the first horror which they had felt, and to change it to a feeling of simple anxiety. Clive was the first to speak.

"Well," said he, as he drew a long breath, " I'd give something to know what all this may mean."

David heaved a very heavy sigh.

" I don't know," said he, dolefully. " I don't understand."

"I wonder if Vernon can have had anything to do with any revolutionary movements. He may have been denounced, and that may have been the reason why he ran away."

"He didn't run away," said David. "Besides, he wouldn't have sacrificed us."

"O, we shan't be sacrificed," said Clive, in a more cheerful tone. "We've been arrested; but when they find out that we've had nothing to do with it, they'll let us go."

"O, I don't think it's anything of that sort," said David. "They don't get up revolutions in Italy now, or conspiracies, for Italy's a free country."

"A queer kind of freedom," said Clive.

"Well, I think," said David, "that there's some other cause for this; and such a cause as may have led to our arrest anywhere — even in New York."

"How?"

"Well — there's Gracie."

"What of her? What's she got to do with it?"

"O, well, she left her aunt, and perhaps her aunt has set the police to find her; and we've been seen with her, so they've arrested us. You know they were trying to find her. Now, I believe they came after her especially, and merely took us because they had seen us with her."

"How could they see us with her?"

"O, easily enough. Why, Clive, Venice is all crammed full of spies."

" What for ? "

" Why, just for nothing at all, and that's the worst of it. But the trouble is, they don't understand yet how to govern in a free country : and though Italy is free, the police, just out of old habit. still keep up their old style of spying, and poking their noses into other people's business, and watching everything. It'll take another hundred years before Italy can be like America — perhaps five hundred."

" I should think so," said Clive.

" Now, in New York," said David, " we could send for a lawyer, and he would get us out on bail."

" Who would give us bail ? "

" I don't know. At any rate he'd get us out ; for no one ever heard of two innocent boys being arrested in America. O, a lawyer could get us out fast enough."

" Well, why mayn't a lawyer get us out of this ? "

" I hope he may, if they'll only let us have one ; but, unfortunately, we seem to be so much in their power that I do not know how we can begin to do anything. You see I asked for the American consul."

" So you did."

" And, you know, they wouldn't take any notice of what I said."

" No," said Clive, mournfully ; " and this shows that they mean to be severe with us. The fact is,

I cannot help thinking that they've made some absurd blunder about it all."

" A blunder ? "

" Yes ; they've mistaken us for some one else."

" That's not unlikely."

" Why, it's very likely indeed. For what earthly reason could they have to arrest a couple of boys like us ? What have we ever done ? Haven't we been as quiet as mice ? Can you imagine a single thing that we have ever done which they could torture into any offence against the laws ? "

" Certainly not," said David. " We've done wrong in one way, of course, but not in a way that the Venetian government could notice. For you see, Clive, we did wrong in leaving Bologna without hearing from Uncle Moses. I can imagine how he must have suffered. We've been enjoying ourselves all along, while he's been tormented with anxiety. Well, our enjoyment's over now, at any rate, and I'm prepared to take this as a sort of punishment for wrong-doing, and bear it like a man."

" O, that's all very well," said Clive ; " but at the same time it is an undeniable fact that no one has any right to keep us here in prison. It's an outrage on the rights of free Americans."

In this way they passed the remainder of the day. Evening came, and their dinner was brought. It consisted of cold meats, with coffee. It was not a bad dinner, and the boys, in spite of their anxiety and trouble, were ravenously hungry. They ate their dinner, therefore, with great satisfaction; and the only fault that they had to find with it was, that there was not quite enough. Then evening deepened into night. They had no lights; so they went to bed, and soon fell fast asleep.

They slept so soundly that they did not awake until their jailer entered with breakfast. Then they arose and partook of their morning meal. When the jailer reappeared, they tried to make known to him, in their broken Italian, the desire which they had to see the American consul; but the jailer either could not or would not understand them. In vain they made use of all their knowledge, not only of the Italian, but even the Latin language. At every new trial the jailer would smile, and nod, and make gestures, which indicated everything but a comprehension of their meaning. It was evident to them both that no help could be looked for in that quarter.

The jailer removed the dishes and departed. Now there arose before them the long, long, dreary day. Their imprisonment began to seem serious, inasmuch as they found themselves utterly helpless, and unable to do a single thing towards gaining a hearing of their case.

" It's a curious way to treat harmless travellers," said Clive; " and it seems to me to be a perfectly horrible violation of the most sacred rights of free Americans."

"O, what's the use of talking of free Americans?" said David, gloomily. "We're Americans, and we're not free, and have no prospect of freedom. How can we say or do anything? We're buried alive here, beyond the reach of our friends, out of their sight, and with no hope of having any communication with them. O, if Vernon would only come back! But he's gone off upon a journey that may be a long one, and who can tell when he'll return? When he does come back, he'll forget all about us: he'll think that we've gone away ourselves, just as we went away from Uncle Moses. I've no confidence in the Venetian police. I'm afraid they keep up something of their old habits of severity, and though they've abolished the torture, still they like to keep people in prison as long as they can."

Clive said nothing in reply. David's despondent frame of mind was communicated to him, and they both were filled with the most gloomy forebodings.

CHAPTER XXIV.

*The Police once more. — An affecting Meeting. — Grand
Reunion at the Hotel Zeno. — Uncle Moses causes a great
Surprise.*

NO sooner had Uncle Moses arrived at Venice,
than he was eager to learn whether anything had been found out about Clive and
David — a feeling which was shared by the others,
and particularly by Miss Lee, who was as anxious
about Gracie as Uncle Moses was for his lost boys.
And so, as soon as possible, Uncle Moses proceeded
to the Police Bureau, accompanied by Frank and
Bob, leaving Miss Lee at the hotel to await their
return.

To their first eager inquiry, the official gave an
answer which filled them with delight.

"Found dem? O, vais: we did finda dems."

"Where?" asked Frank, eagerly.

"O, at de ouse of a friends — an Americano."

"An American! Who is he? What's his name?
Where does he live?"

"Is name, eet ees Vairnon," said the official.

"Vernon. Vernon? I don't know him."

"De signorina dat you name in de telegram, we
did not finda. She gon away."

" Gone !   Where ? "

The official shrugged his shoulders.

" O, she gon away wit Vairnon."

" O, gone away with Vernon.   And the boys —
where were they ?   Did you find them ? "

" O, yais, we dit find em."

" Where are they ?   Will you give us the address ? " asked Frank, eagerly.   " We want to see
them at once — as soon as possible."

" O, yais, you sall see dem as soon as possibile,"
said the official, with a smile.

Frank, who now considered himself well up in
Italian ways, here put some money into the hand
of this smiling functionary, and said, —

" Can't you send some one with us to show us
the place, so that we may find it with the least possible delay ? "

" O, yais," was the reply.   " All aright.   You sall
haf no delay.   Dey ere."

" Here ! " exclaimed Frank.

" O, yais ; ere in dis ouse, secure, an all aright."

" Do you mean to say," cried Frank, " that they
are here in this house ? "

" O, yais, dat ees eet ; an I sall haf dems bote
brought out right away.   You wait un moment."

With these words the official withdrew, leaving
his visitors in a state of delight inexpressible.
Uncle Moses, indeed, felt somewhat shocked at
finding his boys thus turn up in prison, after all
their wanderings ; but the idea of finding them

was of itself so delightful that it overshadowed
everything else, and he awaited the return of the
official with trembling eagerness. Bob was, however, immensely amused at this. He nudged Frank
with his elbow, and said, —

"I say, Frank, I rather think they'll know as
much about Venice as I did, prisons and all; but,
O, isn't it rich to think of the poetic Clive and
sober-sided David turning up here? I say, Frank,
your turn'll have to come. You'll be the next one
here, and then poor Uncle Moses'll have to take
his turn."

They were not left long in suspense; but after a
few minutes the official returned, along with Clive
and David. The joy on both sides was equal, and
was too great for words. They all clung to one
another in a promiscuous manner, and could not
speak. Uncle Moses was too full of happiness to
think of reproaching the runaways, and they were
too full of thankfulness to find any words of excuse
or apology. All these things had to be deferred to
a future occasion.

Before leaving, Frank made a few more inquiries
about Gracie; but Clive told him that he could inform him all about that; so they took their departure, and returned to the Hotel Zeno. On the way
Clive and David told them all about the cause of
Vernon's departure, and of Gracie's journey with
him, which information made them stop at the
telegraph office, and despatch several messages to

Vernon, directed to the various hotels at Verona, and one also to the police, requesting that Vernon be acquainted with Miss Lee's arrival at Venice. They felt certain that some of these messages would reach their destination.

After this they returned to the Hotel Zeno. On the way Clive and David told the whole story of their wanderings, and Uncle Moses told all about his journey after them; and with these explanations were mingled all those expressions of contrition on the one hand, and of forgiveness on the other, which the occasion demanded.

On reaching the Hotel Zeno, they went at once to see Miss Lee, to tell her the news. They found her surrounded by a party of people who were strangers to them, but were evidently the dearest possible friends to Miss Lee. A suspicion came to them as to who these new comers might be, and this was soon confirmed by Miss Lee herself, who introduced to them her brother, Mr. Henry Lee, his wife, and two cousins. They had come to Venice the evening before, and having heard of her arrival, had hastened to welcome her. They had just heard her story, and were, therefore, full of anxiety about Gracie. This anxiety, however, was soon calmed by the information which Uncle Moses gave, and the mention of Vernon's name seemed to carry with it additional assurance that all would be well.

"Vernon," said Mr. Henry Lee. "O, I know

him very well indeed, and his mother, too. She
left Boston some time since to join him here. He
is doing finely, and already has a great reputation
as an artist. He has a most brilliant future before
him. Gracie has certainly fallen among pleasant
friends."

"We found her first," said Clive, proudly. "We
met her in the cars."

"O, you did?" said Mr. Lee; and thereupon he
made Clive tell him all about it. Clive did so, and
told him, in addition, all about their flight from their
uncle, their various wanderings, and final fate.

Mr. Lee laughed more than once, and at length
said, —

"Well, boys, your Uncle Moses, with you, seems
to me like a hen that has hatched a brood of ducks.
After endless trouble with them, she sees them all
take to the water."

"Yes," said Clive, "that's what we did. I suppose coming to Venice may be called taking to the
water."

"Well," said Bob, "I took to the water in real
earnest; but the police were too much for me."

"Yes," said Mr. Lee, "you've had your fling, and
you've suffered for it. For the future you ought
to learn to be more careful. Mind, I'm not giving
you advice. Advice, by itself, is generally of very
little use. Wisdom doesn't come by advice, but
by experience, and you've had an experience which
ought to teach you a good lesson."

The only thing now needed to complete the happiness of all was the return of Gracie; but it was felt that she was in good hands, and that the various telegrams would certainly reach Vernon before he could think of leaving Verona. It was expected that he would receive them that day, and that he would come back by the first train on the following day. Accordingly Frank, Bob, David, and Clive entreated Uncle Moses to let them go to the station and meet them. This request was granted without any demur. Uncle Moses seemed to have lost much of his former anxious timidity. Mr. Lee was desirous of meeting Gracie on her arrival: so he went with them, and at the proper time they all stood awaiting the advent of the train.

In the mean time, as has been shown, Vernon had learned about Miss Lee's departure for Venice with Uncle Moses and Frank and Bob, while the telegrams that he afterwards received confirmed the news in the fullest manner. Although he would have liked to travel all over Italy with Gracie, yet he did not hesitate a moment about returning home; and so, as the party waited in the station-house, the train arrived, and Vernon, with his mother and Gracie, got out.

There was now a very joyous meeting, and Vernon, who, with his mother, accompanied them to the Hotel Zeno, saw Gracie restored to her guardian aunt.

That evening Vernon's home seemed lonely to

him, and he missed the sweet companionship that, for a few happy days, had filled it with sunshine. But Gracie, though no longer a visitor in his house, was still in Venice, and it was the intention of her friends to stay there some time.

All that time was spent by Vernon in the exclusive devotion of himself to Gracie. There were many things to be seen. He revisited the old scenes in company with the whole party, and many new ones. He had many more stories in his manuscript, and these he read to them now under the arcades of palaces, again while floating lazily in the gondola, and yet again in the evening at the Hotel Zeno. They were also often at his house, looking at his pictures or sketches, and seeing the vivid portrayal of the very events which he had been narrating. These days were quite as pleasant to Gracie as the old ones, and in one respect pleasanter, since the anxiety that formerly lay beneath all her enjoyment had now altogether passed away, and there was nothing to think of except the present and its delights.

Uncle Moses did not accompany them in these wanderings. He excused himself on the ground that he had seen enough of sights. So he remained at home in the hotel. As a general thing Miss Lee also remained at home. She, too, declared that she did not care for sight-seeing, and thus it happened that the sudden and sympathetic friendship which had sprung up between Uncle

Moses and Miss Lee in the Amphitheatre at Verona, grew stronger and still more sympathetic at Venice. Uncle Moses was certainly very much changed for the better. He had lost all his former fidgety ways, and seemed no longer to be tormented by that eternal anxiety about the boys which hitherto had been the bane of his existence. The boys were free now to go where they liked. They were always off at an early hour, and never back till dark. All the same to Uncle Moses. He had Miss Lee as his companion, and in her society he seemed to find a grave, calm, quiet satisfaction, that made him feel like a new man.

He was very fond of telling her this.

"You seem," said he, "somehow or nother, to hev made a new man of me. I used to be the forlornedest creetur you ever see, but now I feel like a man, and I'm railly twenty years younger than I was before I met you. An' I railly don't know what to make of it. It beats me, it doos, railly."

At such remarks as these Miss Lee always used to smile upon Uncle Moses so sweetly, that he thought her face like the face of some of the saints that he had seen in cathedrals.

Several weeks passed away in this pleasant fashion, and the Lees were already talking of leaving Venice, when one day Vernon came to see Miss Lee.

His errand was one of a very important kind, and Vernon soon explained it. He informed her that his affections were very deeply engaged with Gracie, and that if she were to leave him now, he would be the most miserable of men; that Gracie had consented to make him happy, and that he had come to her to ask her consent.

Vernon's information was far more circumlocutory than this, and was accompanied with many hesitations and some embarrassments, as is natural in such a delicate matter; but Miss Lee's manner was full of encouragement, and she listened to his words with a smile.

"O, I've seen how it was," said she. "I expected this; but, then, isn't Gracie altogether too young?"

"O, she's young, certainly," said Vernon; "but that is a thing which will be remedied in the course of time."

The end of it was, that Miss Lee gave her consent, but asked Vernon to see her brother about it; which Vernon promised to do.

After his departure, Miss Lee told Uncle Moses, and that good man was moved with feelings of the deepest sympathy for Miss Lee's forlorn condition.

"Dear, dear, dear!" he exclaimed. "So you're goin' to lose her! Why, you'll be quite alone in the world! Now, I s'pose you'll feel dreadful lonely — won't you?"

"O, yes," said Miss Lee.

"Why, it's jest like losin' a darter," said Uncle Moses.

“ O, quite,” said Miss Lee, with a long sigh.

“ And then your brother has his own house, an’ his own fambly matters.”

“ O, yes.”

“ I ben thinkin’ of this for a long time,” said Uncle Moses, after a pause. “ I saw how it was, — it’s allus the way with the young folks, — an’ I thought you’d be lonely, jest like me. Now you know I’m allus lonely.”

“ Are you ? ” said Miss Lee, looking at him in a very sympathetic manner.

“ Allus,” said Uncle Moses. “ Do you ever feel lonely ? I s’pose not.”

“ O, yes,” said Miss Lee.

“ Often ? ” inquired Uncle Moses, in a tender voice.

“ O, always,” said Miss Lee.

“ Dear, dear, dear ! on’y think of that,” said Uncle Moses. “ An’ do you feel very lonely ? ”

“ O, very,” said Miss Lee.

“ So do I,” said Uncle Moses, in a rueful voice ; “ an’ when you go, it’ll be wuss than ever.”

Miss Lee sighed.

Uncle Moses drew nearer, looking at her with meek inquiry. Then he took her hand.

“ Don’t go,” said he, in a low voice. “ Don’t leave me, my dear, dear Miss Lee. Stay with me. I never saw anybody that I liked half so well. It’s true, I’m a leetle old ; but, then, better late than never ; an’ I don’t see how I can live, if I lose you

21

— I don't, railly. Don't leave me. Won't you stay with me, my dear, dear Miss Lee, an' be my own — wife?"

As Uncle Moses was speaking, he drew Miss Lee nearer to him, and the good lady let her head rest on his manly shoulder.

"O, what'll they say!" she ejaculated; and that was all that she said. But this was enough for Uncle Moses. Joy and exultation illumined his eyes.

"Say," said he, in bold, manly, and defiant tones. "Who cares what they say? I don't. You need not. I'll talk to 'em. Don't you fret. It'll be all right. I'll take all the responsibility, an' you will be all my life to me what you have been for these last few weeks — a ministering angel, a heavenly comfort, a sweet companion — everything."

Great was the surprise of the friends of this affectionate pair when they learned the news. Vernon and Gracie were so evidently in love that no one expected anything else of them, though not a single soul had suspected this of Uncle Moses and Miss Lee. But the first surprise soon passed away, and then every one felt very well satisfied. Mr. Lee was glad that his sister had at length met with some one who could make her happy; Gracie was full of affectionate sympathy, and poured forth the warmest congratulations; while all the boys rejoiced over the happiness of their beloved Uncle

Moses. His adventures in foreign parts had brought him little else than misery, but now he would be amply repaid for all that he had endured.

These things caused a further delay in Venice, but at length there came an end to their stay. The two bridegrooms led to the altar their blushing brides, and then, after an affectionate adieu to their friends, the boys departed with Uncle Moses and their new aunt.

AMERICAN BOYS' SERIES

The books selected for this series are all thoroughly American, by such favorite American authors of boys' books as Oliver Optic, Elijah Kellogg, Prof. James DeMille, and others, now made for the first time at a largely reduced price, in order to bring them within the reach of all. Each volume complete in itself.

UNIFORM CLOTH BINDING ILLUSTRATED NEW AND ATTRACTIVE DIES
Price per volume $1.00

1. ADRIFT IN THE ICE FIELDS By Capt. Chas. W. Hall
2. ALL ABOARD or Life on the Lake By Oliver Optic
3. ARK OF ELM ISLAND By Rev. Elijah Kellogg
4. ARTHUR BROWN THE YOUNG CAPTAIN By Rev. Elijah Kellogg
5. BOAT CLUB, THE, or the Bunkers of Rippleton By Oliver Optic
6. BOY FARMERS OF ELM ISLAND, THE By Rev. Elijah Kellogg
7. BOYS OF GRAND PRÉ SCHOOL By Prof. James DeMille
8. "B. O. W. C.", THE By Prof. James DeMille
9. BROUGHT TO THE FRONT or the Young Defenders By Rev. Elijah Kellogg
10. BURYING THE HATCHET or the Young Brave of the Delawares By Rev. Elijah Kellogg
11. CAST AWAY IN THE COLD By Dr. Isaac I. Hayes
12. CHARLIE BELL THE WAIF OF ELM ISLAND By Rev. Elijah Kellogg
13. CHILD OF THE ISLAND GLEN By Rev. Elijah Kellogg
14. CROSSING THE QUICKSANDS By Samuel W. Cozzens
15. CRUISE OF THE CASCO By Rev. Elijah Kellogg
16. FIRE IN THE WOODS By Prof. James DeMille
17. FISHER BOYS OF PLEASANT COVE By Rev. Elijah Kellogg
18. FOREST GLEN or the Mohawk's Friendship By Rev. Elijah Kellogg
19. GOOD OLD TIMES By Rev. Elijah Kellogg
20. HARDSCRABBLE OF ELM ISLAND By Rev. Elijah Kellogg
21. HASTE OR WASTE or the Young Pilot of Lake Champlain By Oliver Optic
22. HOPE AND HAVE By Oliver Optic
23. IN SCHOOL AND OUT or the Conquest of Richard Grant By Oliver Optic
24. JOHN GODSOE'S LEGACY By Rev. Elijah Kellogg

LEE and SHEPARD Publishers Boston

AMERICAN BOYS' SERIES — Continued

25. JUST HIS LUCK By Oliver Optic
26. LION BEN OF ELM ISLAND By Rev. Elijah Kellogg
27. LITTLE BY LITTLE or the Cruise of the Flyaway By Oliver Optic
28. LIVE OAK BOYS or the Adventures of Richard Constable Afloat and Ashore By Rev. Elijah Kellogg
29. LOST IN THE FOG By Prof. James DeMille
30. MISSION OF BLACK RIFLE or On the Trail By Rev. Elijah Kellogg
31. NOW OR NEVER or the Adventures of Bobby Bright By Oliver Optic
32. POOR AND PROUD or the Fortunes or Kate Redburn By Oliver Optic
33. RICH AND HUMBLE or the Mission of Bertha Grant By Oliver Optic
34. SOPHOMORES OF RADCLIFFE or James Trafton and His Boston Friends By Rev. Elijah Kellogg
35. SOWED BY THE WIND or the Poor Boy's Fortune By Rev. Elijah Kellogg
36. SPARK OF GENIUS or the College Life of James Trafton By Elijah Kellogg
37. STOUT HEART or the Student from Over the Sea By Rev. Elijah Kellogg
38. STRONG ARM AND A MOTHER'S BLESSING By Rev. Elijah Kellogg
39. TREASURE OF THE SEA By Prof. James DeMille
40. TRY AGAIN or the Trials and Triumphs of Harry West By Oliver Optic
41. TURNING OF THE TIDE or Radcliffe Rich and his Patient By Rev. Elijah Kellogg
42. UNSEEN HAND or James Renfew and His Boy Helpers By Rev. Elijah Kellogg
43. WATCH AND WAIT or the Young Fugitives By Oliver Optic
44. WHISPERING PINE or the Graduates of Radcliffe By Rev. Elijah Kellogg
45. WINNING HIS SPURS or Henry Morton's First Trial By Rev. Elijah Kellogg
46. WOLF RUN or the Boys of the Wilderness By Rev. Elijah Kellogg
47. WORK AND WIN or Noddy Newman on a Cruise By Oliver Optic
48. YOUNG DELIVERERS OF PLEASANT COVE By Rev. Elijah Kellogg
49. YOUNG SHIPBUILDERS OF ELM ISLAND By Rev. Elijah Kellogg
50. YOUNG TRAIL HUNTERS By Samuel W. Cozzens

LEE and SHEPARD Publishers Boston

PATRIOTIC SERIES FOR BOYS AND GIRLS

"Lives of great men all remind us
We can make our lives sublime."

The volumes included in this series tend to inculcate the spirit of patriotism and good citizenship. The boys and girls of to-day are here made acquainted with the lives and characters of many noble men and women of this and other countries. The information is pleasantly and vividly imparted in the form of popular biography as well as fiction by well-known and popular writers.

UNIFORM CLOTH BINDING NEW AND ATTRACTIVE DIES ILLUSTRATED Price per volume $1.00

1. BOBBIN BOY The Early Life of Gen. N. P. Banks
2. BORDER BOY A Popular Life of Daniel Boone By W. H. Bogart
3. DARING DEEDS OF THE REVOLUTION By Henry C. Watson
4. DORA DARLING or the Daughter of the Regiment By Jane G Austin
5. DORA DARLING AND LITTLE SUNSHINE By Jane G. Austin
6. FATHER OF HIS COUNTRY A Popular Life of George Washington By Henry C. Watson
7. FRIEND OF WASHINGTON A Popular Life of General Lafayette By Henry C. Watson
8. GREAT MEN AND GALLANT DEEDS By J. G. Edgar
9. GREAT PEACEMAKER A Popular Life of William Penn By Henry C. Watson
10. GREAT EXPOUNDER Young Folks' Life of Daniel Webster
11. GOOD AND GREAT MEN Their Brave Deeds and Works By John Frost, LL.D.
12. LITTLE CORPORAL Young Folks' Life of Napoleon Bonaparte By John Frost LL.D.
13. MILL BOY OF THE SLASHES Life of Henry Clay By John Frost
14. NOBLE DEEDS OF AMERICAN WOMEN Edited by J. Clement
15. OLD BELL OF INDEPENDENCE By Henry C. Watson
16. OLD HICKORY Life of Andrew Jackson By John Frost
17. OLD ROUGH AND READY Young Folks' Life of Gen. Zachary Taylor By John Frost, LL.D.
18. PIONEER MOTHERS OF THE WEST Daring and Heroic Deeds of American Women By John Frost, LL.D.
19. PRINTER BOY or How Ben Franklin made his Mark
20. POOR RICHARD'S STORY A Popular Life of Ben Franklin By Henry C. Watson
21. PAUL AND PERSIS or the Revolutionary Struggle in the Mohawk Valley By Mary E. Brush
22. QUAKER AMONG THE INDIANS By Thomas C. Battey
23. SWAMP FOX Life of Gen. Francis Marion By John Frost
24. WOMEN OF WORTH, WHOM THE WORLD LOVES TO HONOR
25. YOUNG INVINCIBLES or Patriotism at Home By I. H. Anderson

LEE and SHEPARD Publishers BOSTON

THE BOUND TO SUCCEED SERIES

By EDWARD STRATEMEYER,

Author of "Under Dewey at Manila," etc.

Three Volumes. Cloth. Illustrated. Price per volume, $1.00.

RICHARD DARE'S VENTURE Or Striking Out for Himself.

OLIVER BRIGHT'S SEARCH Or The Mystery of a Mine.

TO ALASKA FOR GOLD Or The Fortune Hunters of the Yukon.

PRESS OPINIONS OF EDWARD STRATEMEYER'S BOOKS FOR YOUNG PEOPLE.

"In 'Richard Dare's Venture,' Edward Stratemeyer has fully sustained his reputation as an entertaining, helpful, and instructive writer for boys."—*Philadelphia Cail.*

"'Richard Dare's Venture,' by Edward Stratemeyer, tells the story of a country lad who goes to New York to earn enough to support his widowed mother and orphaned sisters. Richard's energy, uprightness of character, and good sense carry him through some trying experiences, and gain him friends."—*The Churchman,* New York.

"A breezy boy's book is 'Oliver Bright's Search.' The author has a direct, graphic style. and every healthy minded youth will enjoy the volume."—*N. Y. Commercial Advertiser.*

"'Richard Dare's Venture' is a fresh, wholesome book to put into a boy's hands." — *St. Louis Post Dispatch.*

"'Richard Dare's Venture' is a wholesome story of a practical boy who made a way for himself when thrown upon his own resources."—*Christian Advocate.*

"It is such books as 'Richard Dare's Venture' that are calculated to inspire young readers with a determination to succeed in life, and to choose some honorable walk in which to find that success. The author, Edward Stratemeyer, has shown a judgment that is altogether too rare in the makers of books for boys, in that he has avoided that sort of heroics in the picturing of the life of his hero which deals in adventures of the daredevil sort. In that respect alone the book commends itself to the favor of parents who have a regard for the education of their sons, but the story is sufficiently enlivening and often thrilling to satisfy the healthful desires of the young reader." *Kansas City Star.*

"Of standard writers of boys' stories there is quite a list, but those who have not read any by Edward Stratemeyer have missed a very goodly thing "—*Boston Ideas.*

For sale by all booksellers, or will be sent, postpaid, on receipt of price by

LEE & SHEPARD, Publishers,
BOSTON.

OLIVER OPTIC'S BOOKS

All-Over-the-World Library. By OLIVER OPTIC. First Series Illustrated. Price per volume, $1.25.

1. **A Missing Million;** OR, THE ADVENTURES OF LOUIS BELGRADE.
2. **A Millionaire at Sixteen;** OR, THE CRUISE OF THE "GUARDIAN MOTHER."
3. **A Young Knight Errant;** OR, CRUISING IN THE WEST INDIES.
4. **Strange Sights Abroad;** OR, ADVENTURES IN EUROPEAN WATERS.

No author has come before the public during the present generation who has achieved a larger and more deserving popularity among young people than "Oliver Optic." His stories have been very numerous, but they have been uniformly excellent in moral tone and literary quality. As indicated in the general title, it is the author's intention to conduct the readers of this entertaining series "around the world." As a means to this end, the hero of the story purchases a steamer which he names the "Guardian Mother," and with a number of guests she proceeds on her voyage. — *Christian Work, N. Y.*

All-Over-the-World Library. By OLIVER OPTIC. Second Series. Illustrated. Price per volume, $1.25.

1. **American Boys Afloat;** OR, CRUISING IN THE ORIENT.
2. **The Young Navigators;** OR, THE FOREIGN CRUISE OF THE "MAUD."
3. **Up and Down the Nile;** OR, YOUNG ADVENTURERS IN AFRICA.
4. **Asiatic Breezes;** OR, STUDENTS ON THE WING.

The interest in these stories is continuous, and there is a great variety of exciting incident woven into the solid information which the book imparts so generously and without the slightest suspicion of dryness. Manly boys will welcome this volume as cordially as they did its predecessors. — *Boston Gazette.*

All-Over-the-World Library. By OLIVER OPTIC. Third Series. Illustrated. Price per volume, $1.25.

1. **Across India;** OR, LIVE BOYS IN THE FAR EAST.
2. **Half Round the World;** OR, AMONG THE UNCIVILIZED.
3. **Four Young Explorers;** OR, SIGHT-SEEING IN THE TROPICS.
4. **Pacific Shores;** OR, ADVENTURES IN EASTERN SEAS.

Amid such new and varied surroundings it would be surprising indeed if the author, with his faculty of making even the commonplace attractive, did not tell an intensely interesting story of adventure, as well as give much information in regard to the distant countries through which our friends pass, and the strange peoples with whom they are brought in contact. This book, and indeed the whole series, is admirably adapted to reading aloud in the family circle, each volume containing matter which will interest all the members of the family. — *Boston Budget.*

OLIVER OPTIC'S BOOKS

Army and Navy Stories. By OLIVER OPTIC. Six volumes. Illustrated. Any volume sold separately. Price per volume, $1.25.

1. The Soldier Boy; OR, TOM SOMERS IN THE ARMY.
2. The Sailor Boy; OR, JACK SOMERS IN THE NAVY.
3. The Young Lieutenant; OR, ADVENTURES OF AN ARMY OFFICER.
4. The Yankee Middy; OR, ADVENTURES OF A NAVY OFFICER.
5. Fighting Joe; OR, THE FORTUNES OF A STAFF OFFICER.
6. Brave Old Salt; OR, LIFE ON THE QUARTER DECK.

"This series of six volumes recounts the adventures of two brothers, Tom and Jack Somers, one in the army, the other in the navy, in the great Civil War. The romantic narratives of the fortunes and exploits of the brothers are thrilling in the extreme. Historical accuracy in the recital of the great events of that period is strictly followed, and the result is, not only a library of entertaining volumes, but also the best history of the Civil War for young people ever written."

Boat Builders Series. By OLIVER OPTIC. In six volumes. Illustrated. Any volume sold separately. Price per volume, $1.25.

1. All Adrift; OR, THE GOLDWING CLUB.
2. Snug Harbor; OR, THE CHAMPLAIN MECHANICS.
3. Square and Compasses; OR, BUILDING THE HOUSE.
4. Stem to Stern; OR, BUILDING THE BOAT.
5. All Taut; OR, RIGGING THE BOAT.
6. Ready About; OR, SAILING THE BOAT.

"The series includes in six successive volumes the whole art of boat building, boat rigging, boat managing, and practical hints to make the ownership of a boat pay. A great deal of useful information is given in this Boat Builders Series, and in each book a very interesting story is interwoven with the information. Every reader will be interested at once in Dory, the hero of 'All Adrift,' and one of the characters retained in the subsequent volumes of the series. His friends will not want to lose sight of him, and every boy who makes his acquaintance in 'All Adrift' will become his friend."

Riverdale Story Books. By OLIVER OPTIC. Twelve volumes. Illustrated. Illuminated covers. Price: cloth, per set, $3.60; per volume, 30 cents; paper, per set, $2.00.

1. Little Merchant.
2. Young Voyagers.
3. Christmas Gift.
4. Dolly and I.
5. Uncle Ben.
6. Birthday Party.
7. Proud and Lazy.
8. Careless Kate.
9. Robinson Crusoe, Jr.
10. The Picnic Party.
11. The Gold Thimble.
12. The Do-Somethings.

Riverdale Story Books. By OLIVER OPTIC. Six volumes. Illustrated. Fancy cloth and colors. Price per volume, 30 cents.

1. Little Merchant.
2. Proud and Lazy.
3. Young Voyagers.
4. Careless Kate.
5. Dolly and I.
6. Robinson Crusoe, Jr.

Flora Lee Library. By OLIVER OPTIC. Six volumes. Illustrated. Fancy cloth and colors. Price per volume, 30 cents.

1. The Picnic Party.
2. The Gold Thimble.
3. The Do-Somethings.
4. Christmas Gift.
5. Uncle Ben.
6. Birthday Party.

These are bright short stories for younger children who are unable to comprehend the Starry Flag Series or the Army and Navy Series. But they all display the author's talent for pleasing and interesting the little folks. They are all fresh and original, preaching no sermons, but inculcating good lessons.

J. T. TROWBRIDGE'S BOOKS

THE TIDE-MILL STORIES. 6 volumes.

Phil and His Friends. By J. T. TROWBRIDGE. Illustrated. $1.25.

The hero is the son of a man who from drink got into debt, and, after having given a paper to a creditor authorizing him to keep the son as a security for his claim, ran away, leaving poor Phil a bond slave. The story involves a great many unexpected incidents, some of which are painful, and some comic. Phil manfully works for a year, cancelling his father's debt, and then escapes. The characters are strongly drawn, and the story is absorbingly interesting.

The Tinkham Brothers' Tide-Mill. By J. T. TROWBRIDGE. Illustrated. $1.25.

"The Tinkham Brothers" were the devoted sons of an invalid mother. The story tells how they purchased a tide-mill, which afterwards, by the ill-will and obstinacy of neighbors, became a source of much trouble to them. It tells also how, by discretion and the exercise of a peaceable spirit, they at last overcame all difficulties.

"Mr. TROWBRIDGE's humor, his fidelity to nature, and story-telling power lose nothing with years; and he stands at the head of those who are furnishing a literature for the young, clean and sweet in tone, and always of interest and value." — *The Continent*.

The Satin-wood Box. By J. T. TROWBRIDGE. Illustrated. $1.25.

"Mr. TROWBRIDGE has always a purpose in his writings, and this time he has undertaken to show how very near an innocent boy can come to the guilty edge and yet be able by fortunate circumstances to rid himself of all suspicion of evil. There is something winsome about the hero; but he has a singular way of falling into bad luck, although the careful reader will never feel the least disposed to doubt his honesty. . . . It is the pain and perplexity which impart to the story its intense interest." — *Syracuse Standard*.

The Little Master. By J. T. TROWBRIDGE. Illustrated. $1.25.

This is the story of a schoolmaster, his trials, disappointments, and final victory. It will recall to many a man his experience in teaching pupils, and in managing their opinionated and self-willed parents. The story has the charm which is always found in Mr. TROWBRIDGE's works.

"Many a teacher could profit by reading of this plucky little schoolmaster." — *Journal of Education*.

His One Fault. By J. T. TROWBRIDGE. Illustrated. $1.25.

"As for the hero of this story, 'His One Fault' was absent-mindedness. He forgot to lock his uncle's stable door, and the horse was stolen. In seeking to recover the stolen horse, he unintentionally stole another. In trying to restore the wrong horse to his rightful owner, he was himself arrested. After no end of comic and dolorous adventures, he surmounted all his misfortunes by downright pluck and genuine good feeling. It is a noble contribution to juvenile literature." — *Woman's Journal*.

Peter Budstone. By J. T. TROWBRIDGE. Illustrated. $1.25.

"TROWBRIDGE's other books have been admirable and deservedly popular, but this one, in our opinion, is the best yet. It is a story at once spirited and touching, with a certain dramatic and artistic quality that appeals to the literary sense as well as to the story-loving appetite. In it Mr. TROWBRIDGE has not lectured or moralized or remonstrated; he has simply shown boys what they are doing when they contemplate hazing. By a good artistic impulse we are not shown the hazing at all; when the story begins, the hazing is already over, and we are introduced immediately to the results. It is an artistic touch also that the boy injured is not hurt because he is a fellow of delicate nerves, but because of his very strength, and the power with which he resisted until overcome by numbers, and subjected to treatment which left him insane. His insanity takes the form of harmless delusion, and the absurdity of his ways and talk enables the author to lighten the sombreness without weakening the moral, in a way that ought to win all boys to his side." — *The Critic*.

J. T. TROWBRIDGE'S BOOKS

THE SILVER MEDAL STORIES. 6 volumes.

The Silver Medal, and Other Stories. By J. T. Trowbridge. Illustrated. $1.25.

There were some schoolboys who had turned housebreakers, and among their plunder was a silver medal that had been given to one John Harrison by the Humane Society for rescuing from drowning a certain Benton Barry. Now Benton Barry was one of the wretched housebreakers. This is the summary of the opening chapter. The story is intensely interesting in its serious as well as its humorous parts.

His Own Master. By J. T. Trowbridge. Illustrated. $1.25

"This is a book after the typical boy's own heart. Its hero is a plucky young fellow, who, seeing no chance for himself at home, determines to make his own way in the world. . . . He sets out accordingly, trudges to the far West, and finds the road to fortune an unpleasantly rough one." — *Philadelphia Inquirer.*

"We class this as one of the best stories for boys we ever read. The tone is perfectly healthy, and the interest is kept up to the end." — *Boston Home Journal.*

Bound in Honor. By J. T. Trowbridge. Illustrated. $1.25.

This story is of a lad, who, though not guilty of any bad action, had been an eye-witness of the conduct of his comrades, and felt "Bound in Honor" not to tell.

"The glimpses we get of New England character are free from any distortion, and their humorous phases are always entertaining. Mr. Trowbridge's brilliant descriptive faculty is shown to great advantage in the opening chapter of the book by a vivid picture of a village fire, and is manifested elsewhere with equally telling effect." — *Boston Courier.*

The Pocket Rifle. By J. T. Trowbridge. Illustrated. $1.25.

"A boy's story which will be read with avidity, as it ought to be, it is so brightly and frankly written, and with such evident knowledge of the temperaments and habits, the friendships and enmities of schoolboys." — *New York Mail.*

"This is a capital story for boys. Trowbridge never tells a story poorly. It teaches honesty, integrity, and friendship, and how best they can be promoted. It shows the danger of hasty judgment and circumstantial evidence; that right-doing pays, and dishonesty never." — *Chicago Inter-Ocean.*

The Jolly Rover. By J. T. Trowbridge. Illustrated. $1.25.

"This book will help to neutralize the ill effects of any poison which children may have swallowed in the way of sham-adventurous stories and wildly fictitious tales. 'The Jolly Rover' runs away from home, and meets life as it is, till he is glad enough to seek again his father's house. Mr. Trowbridge has the power of making an instructive story absorbing in its interest, and of covering a moral so that it is easy to take." — *Christian Intelligencer.*

Young Joe, and Other Boys. By J. T. Trowbridge. Illustrated. $1.25.

Young Joe," who lived at Bass Cove, where he shot wild ducks, took some to town for sale, and attracted the attention of a portly gentleman fond of shooting. This gentleman went duck shooting with Joe, and their adventures were more amusing to the boy than to the amateur sportsman.

There are thirteen other short stories in the book which will be sure to please the young folks.

The Vagabonds: An Illustrated Poem. By J. T. Trowbridge. Cloth. $1.50.

"The Vagabonds" are a strolling fiddler and his dog. The fiddler has been ruined by drink, and his monologue is one of the most pathetic and effective pieces in our literature.